D0826154

Comprehension and Language Arts Skills

Level 4

A Division of The McGraw·Hill Companies

Columbus, Ohio

Table of Contents

Unit 1 Risks and Consequences

Lesson 1 *Mrs. Frisby and the Crow*
Comprehension:
Cause and Effect 2
Grammar and Usage: Nouns 4
Writer's Craft:
Point of View 6

Lesson 2 *Toto*
Comprehension:
Compare and Contrast 8
Grammar and Usage:
Plural and Possessive Nouns 10
Writer's Craft:
Aim/Purpose/Audience 12
Writer's Craft:
Time and Order Words. 14
Writer's Craft:
Place and Location Words 16

Lesson 3 *Sarah, Plain and Tall*
Comprehension:
Author's Point of View 18
Grammar and Usage: Pronouns. . 20
Writer's Craft: Topic Sentences . . 22
Writer's Craft: Paragraph Form . . 24
Writer's Craft: Staying on Topic . . 26

Lesson 4 *Escape*
Comprehension: Sequence 28

Grammar and Usage. Verbs 30
Writer's Craft: Thesis Sentence . . 32
Writer's Craft:
Supporting Details 34
Writer's Craft:
Order of Paragraphs 36

Lesson 5 *Mae Jemison:*
Space Scientist
Comprehension:
Main Idea and Details 38
Grammar and Usage:
What Is a Sentence? 40
Writer's Craft: Exact Words 42
Writer's Craft:
Effective Beginnings
and Endings 44
Writer's Craft: Telling in Time 46

Lesson 6 *Two Tickets to Freedom*
Comprehension:
Drawing Conclusions. 48
Grammar and Usage:
Kinds of Sentences 50

Lesson 7 *Daedalus and Icarus*
Comprehension:
Making Inferences 52
Grammar and Usage: Review . . . 54

Unit 2 Dollars and Sense

Lesson 1 *Starting a Business*
Comprehension:
Main Idea and Details 56
Grammar and Usage:
Types of Sentences 58
Writer's Craft:
Sentence Combining 60

Lesson 2 *Henry Wells and*
William G. Fargo
Mechanics: Capitalization 62
Writer's Craft:
Organizing Expository Writing . . . 64

Lesson 3 *Elias Sifuentes,*
Restaurateur
Mechanics:
Periods and End Punctuation 66
Writer's Craft: Dialogue 68

Lesson 4 *Food From the 'Hood*
Comprehension: Sequence 70

Mechanics: Commas 72
Writer's Craft:
Compare and Contrast 74

Lesson 5 *Business Is Looking Up*
Mechanics: Quotation Marks
and Underlining 76
Writer's Craft:
Developing Expository Writing . . . 78

Lesson 6 *Salt*
Mechanics:
Colons, Semicolons,
and Other Marks 80
Writer's Craft: Plot 82

Lesson 7 *The Milkmaid and*
Her Pail
Grammar, Usage, and Mechanics:
Review 84
Writer's Craft:
Supporting Details 86

Unit 3 From Mystery to Medicine

Lesson 1 *Medicine:*
Past and Present
Mechanics: Apostrophes **88**
Writer's Craft:
Avoiding Wordiness **90**

Lesson 2 *Sewed Up His Heart*
Comprehension:
Drawing Conclusions **92**
Grammar and Usage:
Verb Tenses **94**
Writer's Craft:
Place and Location Words **96**

Lesson 3 *The Bridge Dancers*
Comprehension:
Author's Point of View **98**
Grammar and Usage:
Subject-Verb Agreement **100**
Writer's Craft:
Figurative Language **102**

Lesson 4 *Emily's Hands-On*
Science Experiment
Comprehension:
Fact and Opinion **104**

Grammar and Usage:
Pronoun-Antecedent Agreement . . **106**
Writer's Craft:
Tone of a Personal Letter **108**

Lesson 5 *The New Doctor*
Comprehension:
Making Inferences **110**
Grammar and Usage:
Intensive, Reflexive, and
Demonstrative Pronouns **112**
Writer's Craft:
Aim/Purpose/Audience **114**

Lesson 6 *The Story of Susan*
LaFlesche Picotte
Comprehension:
Cause and Effect **116**
Grammar and Usage:
Adjectives and Adverbs **118**
Writer's Craft:
Time and Order Words **120**

Lesson 7 *The Shadow of a Bull*
Grammar, Usage, and Mechanics:
Review **122**
Writer's Craft:
Aim/Purpose/Audience **124**

Unit 4 Survival

Lesson 1 *Island of the*
Blue Dolphins
Grammar and Usage:
Comparative and
Superlative Adjectives **126**
Writer's Craft:
Organization of
a Narrative Paragraph **128**

Lesson 2 *Arctic Explorer: The*
Story of Matthew Henson
Grammar and Usage:
Comparative and
Superlative Adverbs **130**
Writer's Craft:
Suspense and Surprise **132**

Lesson 3 *McBroom and*
the Big Wind
Comprehension:
Author's Purpose **134**
Grammar and Usage:
Conjunctions and Interjections . . **136**

Writer's Craft: Exaggeration . . . **138**

Lesson 4 *The Big Wave*
Grammar and Usage:
Prepositions **140**
Writer's Craft:
Characterization **142**

Lesson 5 *Anne Frank:*
Diary of a Young Girl
Comprehension:
Author's Point of View **144**
Grammar and Usage:
Double Negatives
and Contractions **146**
Writer's Craft:
Point of View **148**

Lesson 6 *Music and Slavery*
Comprehension:
Main Idea and Details **150**
Grammar and Usage: Review . . **152**
Writer's Craft: Mood **154**

Unit 5 Communication

Lesson 1 *Messages by the Mile*
Comprehension:
Classifying and Categorizing **156**
Grammar and Usage:
Phrases **158**
Writer's Craft:
Developing Persuasive Writing ... **160**

Lesson 2 *We'll Be Right Back*
After These Messages
Comprehension:
Fact and Opinion **162**
Grammar and Usage:
Clauses **164**
Writer's Craft:
Avoiding Wordiness **166**

Lesson 3 *Breaking into Print*
Grammar and Usage:
Direct Objects **168**
Writer's Craft:
Structure of a Business Letter .. **170**

Lesson 4 *Koko's Kitten*
Grammar and Usage:
Fragments, Run-on, Rambling,
and Awkward Sentences **172**
Writer's Craft:
Outlining **174**

Lesson 5 *Louis Braille: The Boy*
Who Invented Books
for the Blind
Comprehension:
Drawing Conclusions **176**
Grammar and Usage:
Agreement in Sentences **178**
Writer's Craft:
Writing a Bibliography **180**

Lesson 6 *My Two Drawings*
Grammar and Usage:
Review **182**
Writer's Craft:
Developing Persuasive Writing ... **184**

Unit 6 A Changing America

Lesson 1 *Early America*
Comprehension:
Classifying and Categorizing **186**
Grammar and Usage:
Parts of Speech **188**
Writer's Craft: End Rhyme **190**
Writer's Craft: Internal Rhyme .. **192**

Lesson 2 *The Voyage of*
the Mayflower
Comprehension:
Making Inferences **194**
Mechanics:
Capitalization and Punctuation .. **196**
Writer's Craft:
Figurative Language **198**

Lesson 3 *Pocohontas*
Grammar and Usage:
Words, Phrases, and Clauses ... **200**
Writer's Craft: Alliteration **202**
Writer's Craft: Assonance **204**

Lesson 4 *Martha Helps the Rebel*
Comprehension:
Compare and Contrast **206**
Grammar and Usage:
Understanding and
Combining Sentences **208**

Writer's Craft: Rhythm **210**
Writer's Craft: Onomatopoeia .. **212**

Lesson 5 *Going West*
Comprehension: Sequence **214**
Grammar and Usage:
Common Irregular Verbs **216**
Writer's Craft: Repetition **218**

Lesson 6 *The California*
Gold Rush
Grammar and Usage:
Past, Present, and
Future Tenses **220**
Writer's Craft:
Charts, Graphs, Tables **222**
Writer's Craft:
Details in Descriptive Writing ... **224**

Lesson 7 *The Golden Spike*
Comprehension:
Cause and Effect **226**
Grammar, Usage, and Mechanics:
Review **228**
Writer's Craft:
Organization of
Descriptive Writing **230**

Cause and Effect

Focus Cause-and-effect relationships help readers understand why events happen in a certain way.

> ▶ A **cause** is why something happens.
> ▶ The **effect** is what happens as a result.
> ▶ Writers use signal words and phrases to identify **cause-and-effect** relationships. These words, which include *because, so, if, then, thus, since, for,* and *therefore,* help readers know what happens and why it happens.

Identify

Look through "Mrs. Frisby and the Crow" for examples of cause-and-effect relationships. For each example, write the event that is the cause and the event that is the effect.

1. **Cause:** _____

_____

Effect: _____

_____

2. **Cause:** _____

_____

Effect: _____

_____

UNIT 1 Risks and Consequences • **Lesson 1** *Mrs. Frisby and the Crow*

▶**Cause and Effect**

COMPREHENSION

Practice

Rewrite each pair of sentences as one sentence showing the cause-and-effect relationship.

3. I could not eat dinner. I ate all the apples.

_____

_____

4. Scruffy bit me. I've been afraid of dogs.

_____

_____

5. I could not find my shoes. I was late.

_____

_____

6. Rachel and Jose put in too much sugar. The recipe did not work.

_____

_____

Apply

Think about a machine you see every day. Write down how you think it works, using cause-and-effect signal words.

_____

_____

_____

_____

UNIT I Risks and Consequences • **Lesson I** *Mrs. Frisby and the Crow*

Nouns

Nouns are words that name persons, places, things, or ideas.

Rule	**Example**
▶ A **common noun** names *any* person, place, thing, or idea.	▶ **student, school, chalkboard**
▶ A **proper noun** names a *particular* person, place, thing, or idea. A proper noun always begins with a capital letter.	▶ **Mr. Stewart, New York City, Empire State Building**
▶ A **concrete noun** names something we can touch or see.	▶ **farmer, water, crow**
▶ An **abstract noun** names something we cannot touch or see, such as an idea or emotion.	▶ **friendship, honesty, happiness**

Read this paragraph. Write *C* over each common noun. Write *P* over each proper noun.

Maryann lived in Venice, Italy, for two years. Venice is a city

in northern Italy. The family had to move because her father

was asked to do a job for his company. Maryann also visited

Great Britain, France, Spain, and many other countries in

Europe.

UNIT 1   Risks and Consequences • **Lesson 1** *Mrs. Frisby and the Crow*

Practice

Read this paragraph. Look at the words in bold type. Underline the words in bold type that are concrete nouns. Circle the words in bold type that are abstract nouns.

Robert heard **laughter** as he walked into the **kitchen.** His mother and **brother** were baking granola. The **smell** coming from the oven was wonderful. Robert's **stomach** growled as he waited for the granola to be done. When the **granola** was finally ready, Robert showed his **happiness** by eating three bars!

Proofread

Read this paragraph. Write the correct lowercase or capital letter above any incorrect ones. Underline the proper nouns. Circle the abstract nouns.

In 2000, the olympics were held in Australia. Athletes from

the United states and many other Countries played many

different sports. Teamwork was important during the

olympics. Many people felt excitement when they

watched their favorite Athletes try to win a Medal.

Point of View

Rule

▸ In every story you read, a narrator tells the story. If the narrator takes part in the story's action, the story is written from a first-person point of view. The narrator uses pronouns such as *I*, *me*, *my*, *we*, *us*, and *our* to tell the story.

▸ If the narrator is an outside observer of the story, the story is written from a third-person point of view. This narrator does *not* take part in the action. The pronouns *he*, *she*, *they*, *them*, and *their* are used to tell the story.

Example

▸ It was as if that tree were calling to me, begging me to climb.

▸ He imagined that the tree was calling to him, begging him to climb it.

 **Try It!** In each sentence, circle the word or words that tell you the point of view. Then write the point of view.

1. Mr. Milston was the best of our neighbors.

   _____

2. It was my idea, but Jason took the credit.

   _____

3. He felt the kitten clinging to him, sinking every tiny claw into

   his leg. _____

4. She peeked around the corner, hoping no one would

   hear her. _____

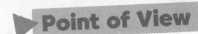

Point of View

Practice

Read the following passage. Then answer the questions about the point of view.

Stefan's palms were cold and sweaty all at once. Why had he ever agreed to do this? Surely the talent show could survive without him. Right now he wasn't sure *he'd* survive. Signing up to audition was one thing. Actually auditioning was another. How would he ever make it across the stage with these shaking knees? He fumbled and almost dropped the drumsticks in his hands. Stefan imagined the headlines: "Drummer with No Rhythm Auditions for Talent Show."

5. In what point of view is this passage written?

_____

6. What words tell you the point of view?

_____

7. What words reveal the character's thoughts and feelings?

_____

_____

_____

Now rewrite the above passage using a different point of view.

_____

_____

_____

_____

WRITER'S CRAFT

Compare and Contrast

Focus Comparing and contrasting helps explain how people, events or things are alike or how they are different.

> ▶ To **compare** means telling how two or more things, events, or characters are alike.
> ▶ To **contrast** means telling how two or more things, events, or characters are different.

Identify

Look through "Toto." Find ways the author compares and contrasts Toto and Suku. Fill in the Venn diagram below with examples from the story. In the left circle, describe Suku. In the right circle, describe Toto. In the middle circle, describe how they are the same.

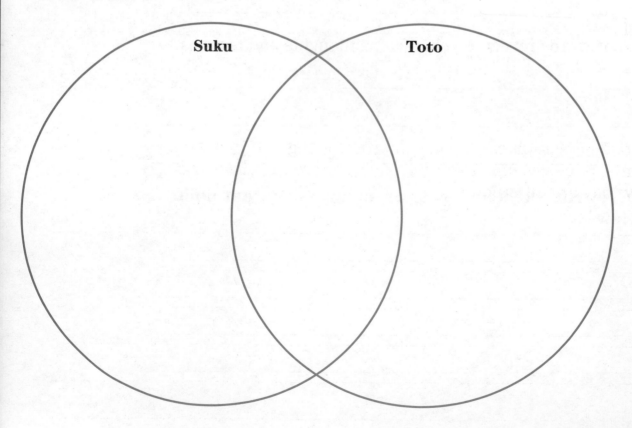

Suku   Toto

▶**Compare and Contrast**

COMPREHENSION

Practice

Read each sentence. Underline the two things that are being compared in each sentence. Write down how they are alike and how they are different.

1. Toto is like Suku.

How are they alike? _____

_____

How are they different? _____

_____

2. Mrs. Frisby is like the Crow.

How are they alike? _____

_____

How are they different? _____

_____

Apply

Write a paragraph comparing and contrasting two things, events, or characters. Describe how they are the same and how they are different.

_____

_____

_____

_____

_____

_____

Plural and Possessive Nouns

A **plural noun** names more than one person, place, thing, or idea.

Rule	**Example**
▶ Many nouns become plural by adding -*s* to the noun.	▶ book, books
▶ For nouns that end in *s*, *x*, *z*, *ch*, or *sh*, add -*es*.	▶ box, boxes bunch, bunches
▶ For nouns that end in a consonant + *y*, change the *y* to *i* and add -*es*.	▶ bunny, bunnies cherry, cherries
▶ For some nouns that end in *f* or *fe*, change *f* to *v* and add -*es*.	▶ knife, knives
▶ For a few nouns that end in *f* or *fe*, add -*s*.	▶ café, cafés
▶ For some nouns, there are no rules for forming plurals. The spelling may be different or the same for both the singular and plural forms.	▶ deer, deer goose, geese
▶ A **possessive noun** shows ownership of things or qualities. To show ownership, add -'*s* to a singular noun or a plural noun that does not end in -*s* or -*es*.	▶ Craig's lunch the children's rooms
▶ Add an apostrophe after the final -*s* to a plural noun that ends in -*s* or -*es*.	▶ the runners' shoes

Read this paragraph. Write the plural form of each word in parentheses.

Africa is one of the seven (continent) _____ in

the world. There are many (country) _____ in

Africa. Along the coasts there are (beach) _____.

Practice

Write the possessive form of each noun in the blank.

1. The homework belonging to Juan is _____
homework.

2. The bicycles belonging to a group of girls are the

_____ bicycles.

3. The toys belonging to a group of children are the

_____ toys.

Proofread

Read this paragraph. If an underlined word is incorrect, write the correct spelling above it.

Cameron went to <u>Nathaniel's</u> house. The two <u>boyes</u> walked

to the bookstore to buy a new book. The change in <u>Camerons'</u>

pockets felt very heavy, and some <u>pennys</u> fell to the ground as

he walked. When they arrived at the store, the <u>boys</u> saw <u>shelfs</u>

stacked with <u>books.</u>

GRAMMAR AND USAGE

UNIT I Risks and Consequences • **Lesson 2** *Toto*

Aim, Purpose, and Audience

Before a writer begins any writing project, it is important to know exactly what her aim, purpose, and audience are.

A writer's aim is the message he or she wants to convey. For example, a writer who tells about a trip she took may want to share a pleasant experience with others.

A writer's purpose may be to inform, to explain, to entertain, or to persuade. For example, a writer may choose to use humor to persuade his readers about something.

The audience is the people who will read the written product.

Try It! **For each writing topic below, tell what the writer's aim might be.**

1. A student complains about menu choices in the school lunchroom.

2. Carla tells about her trip to Yellowstone.

3. Bailey creates a story set in the future.

4. Mike writes instructions for a board game he's designed.

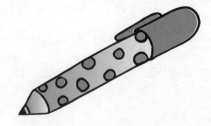

▶ **Aim, Purpose, and Audience**

Practice

Read each paragraph below. Then write the author's purpose: to inform, to explain, to entertain, or to persuade.

5. I thought balancing a gumdrop on the end of my nose was a pretty good idea. What I didn't know was that the gumdrop had just fallen off my sister's gingerbread house. It had fresh glue on it. I balanced it all the way through two songs on the radio.

Purpose: _____

6. If the Elm Street playground is closed, hundreds of families will be affected. Children need a safe place to play. Without the playground they will be forced to use sidewalks and streets for their games. We cannot let the playground be closed.

Purpose: _____

Read the following paragraph. Identify who the audience might be. Then explain your answer.

7. When you enter the school's front door, the office is the second door on the left. Ms. Sandoval, the secretary, can answer any questions you might have. Then, to get to the gymnasium, follow the main hall all the way to the end, then turn right. Enter the gym through the large blue doors.

Audience: _____

_____

WRITER'S CRAFT

Time and Order Words

Rule
▶ There are certain words, called **signal words,** that show **time,** or chronological, order. Some words that show time are *earlier, later,* and *yesterday.*

▶ There are signal words that show **order,** such as a sequence of events or steps in a process. Some words that show sequence are *first, next,* and *finally.*

Example
▶ **Later** that day, I could find my home room, the music room, and the gym without getting lost.

▶ At **first,** I didn't know where to go. There were so many hallways and doorways in this new school.

Read the following passages. In each passage, underline the time and order words.

1. The wild animals seemed to know that a storm was coming. First, the birds got very quiet. Then the squirrels ran to their nest in the oak tree. Meanwhile, even our big, brave cat slid under the sofa, and there he stayed.

2. Today was an odd day. On the way home from school I saw a squirrel sitting on a branch. It looked as if it were sitting there waving at me. That was the first weird thing that happened. The second weird thing happened when I crossed Evan Street. The crossing guard smiled and said, "Funny thing about squirrels, isn't it?" Finally, on my front porch there was a whole pile of acorns. If I didn't know better, I'd think they were a gift from that squirrel.

UNIT 1 Risks and Consequences • **Lesson 2** *Toto*

▶ **Time and Order Words**

Practice

Use time and order words to decide the correct order of details in each set of sentences. Then write the sentences in the correct order.

3. Next, we pushed them into a huge pile. First, we raked the leaves. Then we ran and jumped into the pile.

_____

_____

4. After the dogs, he feeds the rabbits. Then he feeds and waters the dogs. Before Brad goes to school, he has chores to do. First he gets dressed and eats breakfast, of course.

_____

_____

5. Right now I need to go to the grocery store. After lunch you can go next door to play. After I get back from the store, it will be lunch time.

_____

_____

6. Each player reveals a card, in turn, until two matching cards are revealed. That player then turns over a card. Before play begins, roll the die to see who gets the highest number.

_____

_____

_____

WRITER'S CRAFT

Place and Location Words

Place and location words help readers understand where things are or where actions take place. Here are some common place and location words:

about	above	across	along	among	around
at	behind	beside	by	down	into
near	on	out	over	past	through
to	under	up	within	without	outside

In narrative or descriptive writing, writers use place and location words to help readers "see" a setting or the characters' actions. In informative or explanatory writing, place and location words make details or instructions clear.

Underline the place or location word in each sentence.

1. Bicycle tires roll over the stones.

2. Bicycle riders bounce on the seat.

3. Wide eyes look across the handlebars.

4. The riders coast down the hill.

5. As they get near a street, they stop.

6. The lead rider looks around.

► **Place and Location Words**

Practice

Read each sentence starter. Then add a place or location word and any other necessary words to complete the sentence. A sample is done for you.

The boxes were stacked *in the corner of the room.*

7. The space shuttle landed _____

8. Snowflakes floated _____

9. The waters of the river _____

10. The rooster's call awoke _____

11. The Pietro family lives _____

12. The children on the trampoline _____

Choose one wall of your classroom to describe. Start at one side of the wall and describe all objects along the entire length of the wall. Use place and location words so that your readers can see the position of everything on the wall.

_____

_____

_____

_____

_____

_____

_____

_____

WRITER'S CRAFT

Author's Point of View

Focus Every story is told from a specific point of view. Writers must decide on the point of view from which a story is told.

All stories are told through a narrator, which is the person who tells the story. The narrator can tell the story from

▶ the **third-person point of view.** The narrator is an outside observer and uses pronouns such as *he, she,* and *they* when telling the story.

▶ the **first-person point of view.** The narrator is a character in the story and uses pronouns such as *I, me,* and *my* when telling the story.

Identify

Look through "Sarah, Plain and Tall." Find three sentences that show the author's point of view. Write the page number, the sentence, and the point of view in the spaces below.

1. Page: _____ Point of View: _____

Sentence: _____

_____

2. Page: _____ Point of View: _____

Sentence: _____

_____

3. Page: _____ Point of View: _____

Sentence: _____

_____

▶**Author's Point of View**

COMPREHENSION

Practice

Read the following passage. Answer the questions about the author's point of view.

My mom and I planted a flower garden in the vacant lot at the end of the block. We knew it was a risky project because dogs or pranksters might dig up the flowers. But to my mom and me, the risk was worth taking. The colorful flowers added beauty to our neighborhood.

4. What is the author's point of view? _____

5. What words tell you the author's point of view?

_____

Apply

Rewrite the above passage using the third-person point of view.

_____

_____

_____

_____

_____

_____

_____

_____

UNIT I Risks and Consequences • **Lesson 3** *Sarah, Plain and Tall*

Pronouns

A **pronoun** is a word that takes the place of a noun in a sentence. Pronouns that name specific persons or things are called **personal pronouns**. A personal pronoun can replace

Rule	**Example**
▶ a singular or plural subject noun	▶ **The dog** barked. **It** barked.
▶ a singular or plural object noun	▶ The dog barked at **Iris.** The dog barked at **her.**
▶ a singular or plural possessive noun	▶ Here is **Terrell's** book. Here is **his** book.
▶ The pronoun *I* always takes the place of a subject noun. The pronoun *me* always takes the place of an object noun.	▶ **I** talked with Trevor. Trevor talked with **me.**

Try It!

Read this paragraph. The pronouns are missing. Write the correct pronoun in each blank so that the paragraph makes sense.

Joshua and Kaitlyn were sure that the hot-air balloon was

moving faster than _____ thought it should be. Kaitlyn

looked at Joshua and told _____ that _____ wasn't

scared. Joshua said that _____ wasn't scared either.

Although neither one of _____ was scared, _____

both agreed to keep talking to each other. Finally, the pilot of

the balloon said, "It's time for _____ to land."

▶ **Pronouns**

GRAMMAR AND USAGE

Practice

Underline the correct pronoun in parentheses for each sentence.

1. (Her, Mine) papers are on the table.

2. The jacket belongs to (I, me).

3. Blue is (my, me) favorite color.

4. (He, His) is wearing a new tie.

5. (Their, They) shoes are wet.

Proofread

Read this paragraph. If an underlined pronoun is incorrect, write the correct pronoun above it.

   The strange men left their enormous wooden boats and waded toward shore. This was the first time that us had seen these people, and us weren't sure what them wanted. We asked one another, "Who are these men? Why are them here? What are those things in theirs hands?" We shall soon see what it want, me thought.

UNIT I Risks and Consequences • **Lesson 3** *Sarah, Plain and Tall*

Topic Sentences

A topic sentence states the main idea of a paragraph. In many paragraphs, the topic sentence is the first sentence. However, a topic sentence may fall in the middle or at the end of a paragraph. Here are two things to remember about a topic sentence.

A topic sentence should
1. tell what the paragraph is about.
2. state an idea narrow enough to be covered in one paragraph.

Here is a paragraph with a good topic sentence. It makes readers want to know what else is coming.

Example

▶ The transcontinental railroad was almost complete. Two huge engines moved closer and closer. The crowd moved in closer, as well. Promontory Point, Utah, had never seen such a crowd. At last the final rail was in place, the gold and silver spikes were driven, and the noses of the trains touched. It was May 10, 1869.

Read the following topic sentences. Then write what the topic of each paragraph might be.

1. Mountain lions are in the news!

_____

2. I'm going to write about Abraham Lincoln.

_____

3. Hummingbirds are tiny, beautiful birds.

_____

4. Paul's answer made no sense to me.

_____

▶ **Topic Sentences**

Practice

Each of the following paragraphs is missing a topic sentence. Write a topic sentence that tells what each paragraph is about. Make sure each paragraph is indented.

5. _____

Long ago, the Aztecs of Mexico used jewelry to show a person's place in society. Jewelry has been worn for its magical powers and as a way of remembering people. And in East Africa, some people used jewelry as weapons.

6. _____

The food of Mexico has become popular in all parts of the country. Many Mexican words have become part of the English language. Mexican music has influenced American music. And Mexican designs are used in American houses, especially in the Southwest.

7. _____

Milk keeps your bones strong as you grow. Scientists studied the bones of people who drank milk when they were children and teen-agers. The people who drank more milk had healthier, stronger bones. In addition, people who kept on drinking milk as adults continued to have strong bones.

WRITER'S CRAFT

Paragraph Form

A paragraph is usually a group of sentences that tell about the same thing. Sometimes a paragraph can be one sentence in some forms of writing, such as narrative writing.

A topic sentence states the main idea of a paragraph. The topic sentence is often the first sentence in the paragraph. However, it may fall in any position in the paragraph.

Other sentences provide details that support the main idea. Those details may be facts, examples, reasons, or simply descriptive information. The kinds of details depend on the kind of writing.

Example

▶ Tam conducted her experiment with great care. First, she got all of the supplies. Then she got Fluffy and set her on a bench. Fluffy stood and sniffed the supplies. One of the items was a bowl of special cat food. Fluffy began gobbling. The experiment was a success.

 **Underline the topic sentence in each paragraph.**

1. Carrots have many uses. People eat them raw, either alone or in salads. Many recipes call for carrots in soups and stews. Carrots can also be boiled and eaten alone. And can you imagine roasting, grinding, and using a carrot as a substitute for coffee?

2. Only some of the things you might have heard about piranhas are true. For example, most people know that piranhas are meat-eaters with sharp teeth. However, they seldom have attacked humans. Normally, piranhas travel alone, eating smaller fish or seeds in the water. Only sometimes do piranhas swim together. When they do, they *may* attack a larger fish or water animal.

UNIT 1 Risks and Consequences • **Lesson 3** *Sarah, Plain and Tall*

▶Paragraph Form

Practice

The following sentences form a paragraph. Decide what order the sentences should follow. Put the topic sentence first. Then organize the supporting sentences in a logical order. Write the complete paragraph in the space provided.

The five oldest tunnels are for trains.

And from 1937 to 1957, the last and largest of the tunnels for automobiles was built.

These rapid transit tunnels opened between 1908 and 1910.

Seven tunnels for trains and automobiles provide a vital link between Manhattan Island and New Jersey.

It has three "tubes" that each allow for two lanes of automobile traffic.

Tens of thousands of people pass through these tunnels—and under the Hudson River—each day.

In 1927, a tunnel for automobiles opened.

_____

_____

_____

_____

_____

_____

_____

_____

_____

_____

WRITER'S CRAFT

Staying on Topic

Staying on topic means including information only about your main idea. To stay on topic, don't use unnecessary words. Do not include thoughts or ideas that don't relate to the main idea. How do you know if you're staying on topic? When you look at the first draft of a piece of writing, make sure *you* know what the main idea of each paragraph is. Then look at each sentence and ask yourself, "Does this sentence tell more about the main idea, or does it talk about something else?"

Example

▶Many nations ~~and groups of people~~ were interested in settling or controlling what is now California. ~~The nations of~~ Spain and England sent explorers who sailed along the coast during the 1500s. ~~Many places in California have Spanish names.~~ Later, Russia expanded its Alaskan fur-trading business all the way down into California. And in 1822, California came under the control of Mexico.

Try It!   **Read the following paragraph. Find the words or phrases that are unnecessary. Cross them out of the paragraph.**

1.   The restaurant kitchen was like a battleground. It seemed as if there were a dozen servers whooshed in and out with huge trays. The head chef moved from pot to pot on the stove. He spent summers at Myrtle Beach. At the same time, he watched everything else that happened in the room. All of the other kitchen workers hurried and dashed about between coolers and food preparation areas. There was a constant rattle and rumble as slicers and choppers created diced carrots, minced onions, and chopped peppers.

▶**Staying on Topic**

Practice

In each of the following paragraphs, the writers had trouble staying on topic. Tell how to improve each paragraph.

2.   Though penguins are birds, they have special characteristics. Penguins' feathers are different from those of most birds. They are made to keep the penguins warm, even in the water. Penguins' bodies allow them to glide through the water. They use their flippers to steer. Other birds build nests in trees.

_____

_____

3.   Making a nice greeting card is the easiest thing in the world. First, fold a sheet of construction paper in half. Carefully cut a simple shape out of the front of the card. It might be a flower, a heart, or just a geometric shape. Once I made a neat card with triangles on it. Then, on the inside of the card, glue or tape a different colored piece of construction paper over the cut-out section. Write a simple message on the inside, and your card is done.

_____

_____

4.   Cold weather in Florida is bad news. Hundreds of orange growers depend on Florida's warm weather. If the temperature goes below freezing, the farmers can lose an entire crop of oranges. Some tourists don't like oranges. Losing a crop means a shortage of oranges. And then we all pay a higher price for oranges and orange juice. That's the bad news.

_____

_____

WRITER'S CRAFT

Sequence

Focus   Sequence is the order of events in a story. Writers often use signal words called time and order words to help readers follow the action in a story.

Time and order words show

▸ the **order** in which events take place. Words such as *first*, *then*, *so*, *when*, and *finally* show order.

▸ the passage of **time** in a story. Words such as *spring*, *tomorrow*, and *morning* show time.

Identify

Look through "Escape." Find sentences with time and order words. Write the words along with a *T* next to the word if it shows time and *O* if it shows order. Then explain how these words help you understand the sequence of events in the story.

1. Word: _____ Time/Order: _____

2. Word: _____ Time/Order: _____

3. Word: _____ Time/Order: _____

4. Word: _____ Time/Order: _____

5. Word: _____ Time/Order: _____

How do these words help you understand the sequence of events in the story?

_____

_____

_____

_____

Sequence

COMPREHENSION

Practice

Read the following passages. In the first passage, fill in the
spaces with words that signal time. In the second passage, fill
in the spaces with words that signal order.

_____ the bank is open from 9:00 A.M. to

5:00 P.M. It closes at 3:00 P.M. _____. _____
is a holiday, so the bank will be closed all day.

The _____ stop on the tour was the old Post

Office. _____ we visited the theatre. _____

lunch we saw the library. _____ we visited the
museum.

Apply

Write a short paragraph about an ordinary day in your life.
Use time and order words in your paragraph.

_____

_____

_____

_____

_____

_____

_____

_____

Verbs

A **verb** is a word that shows an action or expresses a state of being. Different types of verbs show or express different things.

Rule	**Example**
▶ An **action verb** shows what the subject does. The action can be seen or unseen.	▶ Molly **thought** about her idea.
▶ A **linking verb** does not show action. Linking verbs connect the subject of a sentence with a noun or adjective that renames or describes the subject.	▶ Austin **is** a very good golfer.
▶ A **helping verb** helps the main verb show when an action occurred or will occur, or what state of being is, was, or will be.	▶ Megan **will go** to the party.

Read this paragraph. Circle the action verbs.

In 1977, scientists sent two spaceships to Jupiter. Although the ships traveled very quickly, they took over a year to reach the planet. Thick clouds cover Jupiter. Many moons move around it. Scientists think that meteors crashed into the moons billions of years ago. These meteors made big craters on each moon.

UNIT I Risks and Consequences • **Lesson 4** *Escape*

▶Verbs

GRAMMAR AND USAGE

Practice

Look at the underlined verb in each sentence. Write *L* if the verb is a linking verb. Write *H* if the verb is a helping verb.

1. Jupiter <u>is</u> one of the largest planets in the solar system.

2. No one <u>has</u> seen the surface of the planet before.

3. Jupiter's Great Red Spot <u>seems</u> motionless.

4. A person <u>would</u> weigh more on Jupiter than on Earth.

5. The spaceships took many pictures so scientists <u>might</u> learn more about Jupiter.

6. Scientists <u>are</u> still puzzled about Jupiter.

Proofread

Read this paragraph. Write the word *action, linking*, or *helping* above each bold word to describe what kind of verb it is.

Jupiter **spins** faster than Earth. Powerful winds **swirl** around the planet. The center of Jupiter **is** extremely hot. If Jupiter **were** hollow, the planet Earth **could** fit inside it more than 1300 times. Volcanoes on one of Jupiter's moons **erupt** often. Scientists also **believe** there **might** be ice on some of the moons.

Thesis Sentence

A thesis sentence states the topic of a piece of writing. It is like a topic sentence in a paragraph because both state the main idea. However, unlike a topic sentence, a thesis sentence states the main idea of an **entire** piece of writing, not just a single paragraph. It lets readers know what to expect.

A thesis sentence should

1. be stated at the beginning of the paper, but it does not need to be the first sentence of the opening paragraph.

2. briefly state what the paper is about and what subtopics will be covered.

Some forms of writing, such as narrative and descriptive writing, do not need a thesis sentence.

Example

▶ Oranges are good to eat because they contain vitamins and minerals that keep bodies strong and healthy.

 **Rewrite each sentence as a thesis sentence.**

1. In this paper I'll try to convince you that cross-country skiing is better than downhill skiing.

   _____

2. Cats are playful creatures, and they make great pets as long as you are willing to take care of them properly.

   _____

3. At the market, you can find nearly any kind of fresh food.

   _____

Thesis Sentence

Practice

Each of the following paragraphs is part of a larger piece of writing. Write a possible thesis sentence for each paragraph. If none, write <u>none</u> and explain why.

4. Mr. Loria always liked to give us choices. For example, one day he gave us topic choices for a story. We could write a story titled "Boom" or one titled "It Happened at Noon." Another time he gave us a choice between reading a play or seeing it performed. That was an easy choice!

_____

_____

5. Can you imagine a world without cars? One author has written a new story set in a world with no cars. In the story, cars have been banned because of pollution. Personal space bubbles replace the cars. Traffic jams and finding a parking space are no longer a problem.

_____

_____

6. On the mantle were pictures of Uncle Peter's family. Beside the lamp was a box of pictures from Aunt Susanna. Frames containing me, my mom and dad, and my two brothers stood in a row on the coffee table. In the rocking chair sat Grandma. She liked to have her whole family around her.

_____

_____

WRITER'S CRAFT

UNIT I Risks and Consequences • **Lesson 4** *Escape*

Supporting Details

A good paragraph has two elements. It has a main idea, stated in a topic sentence. The rest of the paragraph, then, consists of sentences that contain supporting details. Those details tell more about the main idea.

Supporting details might be reasons, examples, description, or facts. Different kinds of writing require different kinds of details.

Examples

▶**Reasons:** American consumers must cut down on what they throw away. Trash disposal is becoming a vital issue. Landfills are filling up. Land for new landfills is hard to find. The land is needed for farming or for housing. Where can our trash go next?

▶**Description:** It was one of those autumn days that makes it clear that summer is over. We could hardly hear over the roaring. The branches in the huge maples whipped violently in the wind. Drying leaves swirled, unhappy to be letting go. Our leaf pile was pitiful. The wind snatched half of every rake full, so our progress was slow.

 **Read the following paragraph. Underline the main idea. Then identify two supporting details in the paragraph. Write them below.**

Casey decided that he wanted to know more about birds. First he got some bird books from the library. Then he made a feeder from a plastic bottle and a hanger. He hung the feeder near the patio in the backyard. When he was done, Casey found a comfortable spot where he could sit and watch the sparrows, finches, and jays that came to eat.

Supporting details: _____

_____

Supporting Details

Practice

Read each paragraph below. Then answer the questions that follow.

1. (1) Corn is put to use in so many ways. (2) We eat the grain, or kernels, as cooked vegetables, of course. (3) Kernels are also used to make breakfast cereals and some breads. (4) Cornstalks are chopped up and fed to cattle and hogs. (5) Corn or corn oil is also an ingredient in surprising products, such as paint, medicines, and even paper goods.

What sentence states the paragraph's main idea?

_____

What sentences contain supporting details?

_____

Are the supporting details in this paragraph reasons, description, or facts?

_____

2. (1) The students at Lewis Avenue School are in danger. (2) Many students cross the street at the corner of Lewis Avenue and Fourth Street. (3) It is a busy intersection. (4) To make matters worse, motorists don't always come to a complete stop at the stop sign. (5) A stoplight at the intersection would force motorists to stop and give students time to cross the street safely.

What sentence states the paragraph's main idea?

_____

What sentences contain supporting details?

_____

Are the supporting details in this paragraph reasons, description, or facts?

_____

WRITER'S CRAFT

Order of Paragraphs

Depending on your purpose and audience, certain forms of writing should include three parts: an introduction, a body or middle, and a conclusion.

▶ **Introduction:** The writer tells what the piece is about and catches readers' interest.

▶ **Body or middle:** The writer presents most of the information in a logical manner. The body is usually the longest part of a piece.

▶ **Conclusion:** The writer ties together his or her ideas. The conclusion may contain a summary of those ideas, but it should not simply repeat the ideas.

Writers use sentences and special words, such as transition words, to help readers understand the connection between paragraphs in a piece of writing. Those sentences and words also let readers know what's coming next.

Read the following paragraphs from a report. The first is an introduction. The second is the conclusion. Using proofreading marks, revise the conclusion to make it better.

If ever there was a state for farming, Iowa is it. Its great expanse of prairie has plenty of streams and rivers. It also has a deep layer of good growing soil called loam. That soil is the foundation for a number of important crops.

In spite of Iowa's thriving cities, the state's image as a farming state looms large. And there is good reason for that. Judging by corn alone, Iowa's role as a vital producer is certain. Sensible land use and smart crop production methods will ensure that Iowa continues to provide for all of us.

Order of Paragraphs

Practice

Read the paragraphs. Then answer the questions that follow.

The safety of our children is important to all of us. That is why we must replace some of the playground equipment at Owen Elementary. Certain issues regarding the playground equipment have come to the attention of the Grounds Committee.

Most of the current playground equipment is more than 20 years old. It was installed when the school was built. Though it is in good repair, safety standards have changed. In particular, the merry-go-round and the jungle gym pose serious risks to the children's safety.

We must replace this equipment for the sake of our children. The Grounds Committee is holding an open meeting on Thursday, April 8th, at 6:30 p.m. Please attend and voice your support. Let's all work together.

1. What is the main idea?

_____

_____

2. What phrase or sentence in the introduction hints at what is discussed in the body?

_____

_____

3. What sentence in the conclusion restates or summarizes the main idea?

_____

_____

Main Idea and Details

Focus The main idea is what a paragraph is about. Often, a writer provides a clear topic sentence at the beginning of a paragraph.

> ▶ The **main idea** is the most important point the writer makes in a paragraph. The main idea tells what the whole paragraph is about.
> ▶ **Details** are bits of information in the sentences of a paragraph that support the main idea.

Identify

Find two paragraphs in "Mae Jemison: Space Scientist" that have a clearly stated main idea. Write the page number, main idea, and two details from each paragraph.

1. Page: _____ Main Idea: _____

_____

Detail: _____

_____

Detail: _____

_____

2. Page: _____ Main Idea: _____

_____

Detail: _____

_____

Detail: _____

_____

▶ **Main Idea and Details**

COMPREHENSION

Practice

Read the paragraph. Underline the main idea. In the spaces, write two sentences with details that support the main idea.

Casey decided that he wanted to know more about birds. First he got some bird books from the library. Then he made a feeder from a plastic bottle and a hanger. He hung the feeder near the patio in the backyard. When he was done, Casey found a comfortable spot where he could sit and watch the woodpeckers, finches, and other birds that came for food and water.

Detail: _____

_____

Detail: _____

_____

Apply

Write a paragraph about Mae Jemison. State your main idea in the first sentence. Add sentences with details that support the main idea.

_____

_____

_____

_____

_____

_____

_____

What Is a Sentence?

A sentence expresses a complete thought. The first word in a sentence is always capitalized, and the sentence has end punctuation. Every sentence has two parts—a **subject** and a **predicate.**

Rule	Example
▶ The **simple subject** names who or what does or is something in a sentence. The simple subject and any words that describe it are called the **complete subject.**	▶ **Elena** cleaned her room.
▶ The **simple predicate** of a sentence tells what the subject does or is. The simple predicate, or verb, and any words that describe it, are called the **complete predicate.**	▶ We **went swimming in the lake.**
▶ A **compound subject** is two or more subjects that have the same predicate in a sentence.	▶ **John and Erica** live in two different cities.
▶ A **compound predicate** is two or more predicates that have the same subject in a sentence.	▶ The dog **walked around the room and sniffed the furniture.**
▶ The verb in the predicate agrees in number with the subject in a sentence.	
• subject-verb agreement with a simple subject	▶ John lives in a city.
• subject-verb agreement with a compound or plural subject	▶ John and Erica live in a city. They live in a city.

UNIT I Risks and Consequences • **Lesson 5** *Mae Jemison: Space Scientist*

▶ **What Is a Sentence?**

Read this paragraph. Circle the complete subject in each sentence. Underline the complete predicate in each sentence.

California has several interesting places to visit. Death Valley is a desert. The Death Valley region is home to many wildflowers and animals. San Diego has one of the world's largest zoos. Sacramento is the capital of California.

Practice

Read this paragraph. Underline the compound subject or compound predicate in each sentence. Write *CS* above the compound subjects and *CP* above the compound predicates.

Many things come from California. Almonds, dates, and olives are grown there. Movies and TV shows are also made there. People ski in the mountains and swim in the ocean.

Proofread

Read this paragraph. Circle the complete subject in each sentence. Underline the complete predicate in each sentence. Write *CS* above any compound subjects and *CP* above any compound predicates.

David began to take tennis lessons. He learned how to hit the ball and how to hold his racket. David and his brother practiced for many hours each day. His coach told David that he was ready for his first tennis tournament. David played hard and served the ball well. He won the tournament.

GRAMMAR AND USAGE

Exact Words

Good writers use exact words to express things and actions clearly and to help readers understand their writing. General words do not create pictures the way exact words do.

Here are some examples of sentences with general words and sentences with exact words. Notice how much more interesting the second set of sentences is.

Sentences with General Words	**Sentences with Exact Words**
He opened the door.	He pushed open the heavy door.
The dog went across the field.	The collie raced across the field.

Make a check mark in front of the sentences that contain exact words. Revise the sentences that contain general words. Use more exact nouns, verbs, or descriptive words to make the sentences more vivid.

1. _____ Sue dropped a tiny spot of glue onto the blue cardboard.

    _____

2. _____ The rain felt cold on my face.

    _____

3. _____ Mrs. Sonder walked to the front of the room.

    _____

4. _____ The liquid in the test tube was bright green and a little cloudy.

    _____

Practice

Each sentence below contains general words. Replace general words with exact words, or add exact words to improve each sentence. Write your new sentence in the space provided. Remember to think about the picture you want to create in readers' minds.

5. She walked into the office.

_____

6. I bounced a ball on the sidewalk.

_____

7. The trees were pretty.

_____

8. The cat looked at the dog.

_____

9. The room was full of stuff.

_____

10. A car went past.

_____

11. My teacher talked about the science experiment.

_____

12. Her messy writing was hard to read.

_____

WRITER'S CRAFT

Effective Beginnings and Endings

The **beginning** of a story or article might be the most important part. The beginning is where a writer grabs a reader's attention and is where a reader decides whether to keep reading. Here are some techniques for writing an effective beginning.

Technique	**Example**
▶ Use descriptive details.	▶ The blazing light in the windows flashed as Ted watched. Strange shapes rose up in the flickering light.
▶ Introduce a problem.	▶ Once we got to the beach, nothing went right.
▶ Use dialogue.	▶ "You *said* you would go." J.C. had done it again. He always makes promises he can't keep.
▶ Ask a question.	▶ Have you ever wondered what's at the center of a pearl?
▶ Use an anecdote, or personal story.	▶ When Mr. DiPietro met me at the door in a jogging suit and invited me to run along with him during the interview, I knew I was not dealing with the average 80-year-old man.

The **ending** of a story or article is also important. At the end of a story, the characters' problems need to be solved. The ending should make sense in terms of the story. Sometimes a surprise ending that *is* logical is a great way to end a story.

In an article, the ending should summarize the article's main idea. Writers should not introduce any new ideas in the final paragraph of an article. A good ending leaves readers with something to think about.

WRITER'S CRAFT

► **Effective Beginnings and Endings**

 **Try It!**   **Place a check mark in front of each effective beginning.**

1. ____ The other day I went to the zoo and saw the gorillas and koalas.

2. ____ The doctor's face was pale and tight when he came out of my sister's room.

3. ____ *Incredible* is the best word I can think of to describe Sang Hun's new sculptures.

4. ____ Arthur Mitchell was born in 1934 in New York City.

Practice

Identify each of the following passages as a beginning or an ending. If a sentence is the beginning for a story or article, tell what technique the writer is using.

5. I was hopeless. My experiment was a mess. I knew my chances of passing this unit were slim. That's when I noticed the liquid bubbling in my beaker. Something strange was happening.

Beginning or Ending? _____

Technique: _____

6. I smelled doughnuts all the way through math class. It was the good, fried kind, not the baked ones. I could even smell the warmth of them. This was very odd. It's not as if the cooks in the cafeteria were likely to be making fresh doughnuts.

Beginning or Ending? _____

Technique: _____

UNIT 1   Risks and Consequences • **Lesson 5** *Mae Jemison: Space Scientist*

Telling in Time Order

Writers often tell about events in the order in which they happened. To help readers follow along, writers use signal words. Signal words that tell when something happened are called time words. Signal words that show the order in which things happened are called order words. Here are some examples of time and order signal words.

Time Words   **Order Words**

yesterday, afternoon, winter   first, then, later, meanwhile, after

Telling events in time order is important when you write a story. It's also important when you are writing a history report or telling about an experiment you've done.

 **Identify the time or order word in each sentence. Write the word in the space following the sentence. Then tell whether the word is a time word or an order word.**

1. We go to the school library only on Tuesdays.

_____

2. While we're in the library, our teacher eats her lunch.

_____

3. Then we go to the cafeteria to eat our own lunches.

_____

4. After recess, we're back in our classroom for math.

_____

5. If you visit tomorrow, you'll see our shape museum.

_____

6. I brought a cylinder and two cubes for the museum last week.

_____

▶ **Telling in Time Order**

Practice

The instructions below do not include any order words. Rewrite the passage, adding order words to make the instructions more clear.

7.　Turn left at the corner. Go down the block and past the playground. Turn left at the stoplight. Turn right at the next corner. Take another left on 17th Street, and you'll see my blue house ahead and on the right.

_____

_____

_____

The following sentences tell part of a story, but they are mixed up. Decide in what order the sentences go. (Use the time and order words to help you.) Then write the paragraph in the space provided.

8.　After the last exercise, we were allowed to talk for a few minutes before breakfast.
　　At first light, the bell woke us up.
　　That was the best part of the day at Camp Jupiter.
　　The lines of people in striped pajamas always made me dizzy, but I stretched and moved up and down like everyone else.
　　We rolled out and lined up for morning exercises.

_____

_____

_____

_____

_____

WRITER'S CRAFT

Drawing Conclusions

Focus Drawing conclusions helps readers get more information from a story.

> ▶ **Drawing conclusions** means taking small pieces of information, or details, about a character or story event and using them to make a statement about that character or event.
>
> ▶ The conclusion may not be stated in the text but should be supported by details from the text.

Identify

Look through "Two Tickets to Freedom" for details you can use to draw conclusions. Choose and write two different groups of details from the story and the page number. Then write the conclusion for each.

1. Page: _____ Detail: _____

_____

Detail: _____

_____

Conclusion: _____

2. Page: _____ Detail: _____

_____

Detail: _____

_____

Conclusion: _____

▶ **Drawing Conclusions**

Practice and Apply

Read the paragraph and draw a conclusion. Write the details you used to draw your conclusion.

For weeks, Marco and Allison talked about getting a pet. Marco wanted a dog for protection, but Allison felt that cats made better companions. Marco argued that a dog was the best choice because he and Allison worked all day. The dog would bark if someone approached the house, which would help prevent a robbery. Allison felt that a cat would be a better choice because it could be left home all day more easily than a dog. One day, Allison went shopping. When she returned home, she heard barking in the house.

Conclusion: _____

_____

_____

_____

Detail: _____

_____

_____

Detail: _____

_____

_____

COMPREHENSION

UNIT I Risks and Consequences • **Lesson 6** *Two Tickets to Freedom*

Kinds of Sentences

There are four kinds of sentences that writers use to give readers different information.

Rule

▶ A **declarative sentence** makes a statement and ends with a period.

▶ An **exclamatory sentence** expresses strong feeling or emotion and ends with an exclamation point.

▶ An **interrogative sentence** asks a question and ends with a question mark.

▶ An **imperative sentence** makes a request or gives a command. Usually, imperative sentences end with a period.

Example

▶ Our baseball team won the championship.

▶ Peas are disgusting!

▶ Are we going to the movie theater?

▶ Line up along the right side of the hallway.

 **Try It!**

Read each sentence. Identify the kind of sentence that each one is. Write your answer in the blank.

1. Washington, D.C., is the capital of the United States.

    _____

2. What is your dog's name? _____

3. Do I have to go to bed now? _____

4. The water in the lake is freezing! _____

5. Please fold the laundry. _____

Comprehension and Language Arts Skills

UNIT I   Risks and Consequences • **Lesson 6** *Two Tickets to Freedom*

▶ **Kinds of Sentences**

Practice

Write the correct punctuation at the end of each sentence and identify the kind of sentence that each one is.

6. Many people want to protect the environment ____

_____

7. Can saving electricity help Earth ____

_____

8. Please shut off the light when you leave the room ____

_____

9. Watch out for that spill _____

10. Wash out the bottles before you recycle them ____

_____

11. The ozone layer has been damaged by pollution ____

_____

12. Did you throw away your trash _____

Proofread

Read this story. Write the correct punctuation mark at the end of each sentence.

"Get out of my room ____" Danny's little brother had

been playing in Danny's room even though he wasn't

supposed to ____ "Why don't you go mess up your own

stuff, Paul ____"

Making Inferences

Focus Readers make inferences about characters and events to understand the total picture in a story.

> An **inference** is a statement a reader makes about a character or event from a story. To make an inference, the reader uses
> ▶ **information** from the story, such as examples, facts, reasons, and descriptions.
> ▶ **personal experience or knowledge,** which is the memories and experiences you bring to the story.

Identify

Daedalus and Icarus build wings to escape from King Minos' tower. Choose one of the characters and write an inference on how they felt about this decision. Write the information from the story and the personal experience you used to make the inference.

Character: _____

Inference: _____

_____

Information from the story: _____

_____

_____

Personal Experience: _____

_____

_____

_____

UNIT I   Risks and Consequences • **Lesson 7** *Daedalus and Icarus*

Practice

Read the following paragraph. Then make an inference
by answering the questions.

    Harry's father and mother would be angry when they saw
the table even though Harry had not meant to break it. He
accidently fell on the table while tossing a football in the
house. Harry looked at the broken pieces scattered around
the room. He knew the table could not be fixed.

1. What did Harry do: _____

_____

2. Is Harry worried? Why? _____

_____

3. Can Harry fix the table? Why? _____

_____

Apply

Write a paragraph that continues the above story about Harry
and the table. Include the inferences you made and add
information that will let your readers make new inferences.

_____

_____

_____

_____

_____

_____

_____

COMPREHENSION

Review

Nouns

Circle all proper nouns. Underline all common nouns. Write *C* over all concrete nouns. Write *A* over all abstract nouns.

1. Sean went to San Francisco to visit his cousin.

2. Ryan turned in his project and felt pride about his work.

3. Leslie appreciated the kindness of others when she was sick.

Write the correct plural and/or possessive noun in the blank.

4. The shoes of the women are the _____ shoes.

5. The race of the three athletes is the _____ race.

6. How many _____ (bunch) of hay will the

   _____ (pony) eat?

Pronouns and Verbs

Correct the underlined pronouns. Draw an *X* through the verbs.

Me went to the movies yesterday. The line was long. It took

me twenty minutes to find a seat in the theater. Me put your

snacks on the seat. People knew the seat was my. Someone

told me the movie might be scary. These comment was not

true. Her was the best movie I had seen in a long time.

►**Review**

▶ **What Is a Sentence?**

Circle the complete subject in each sentence. Underline the complete predicate. Write *CS* above any compound subjects. Write *CP* above any compound predicates.

7. Companies use advertising to sell their products.

8. Newspapers, magazines, and TV are three places where people can see ads.

9. Ads give people information and tell them to buy things.

10. Ashton and Patrick read the ad carefully and bought a new video game.

▶ **Kinds of Sentences**

Write the correct punctuation at the end of each sentence and identify the kind of sentence that it is.

11. Please be careful on your way to the park ____

_____

12. How long do you think you'll be there ____

_____

13. The new kickball field opened yesterday ____

_____

14. Oh, no _____ It's beginning to rain ____

_____

15. Maybe you'll be able to play kickball tomorrow ____

_____

GRAMMAR AND USAGE

Main Idea and Details

Focus Writers use a main idea and details to make their point clear in a paragraph.

> ▶ The **main idea** is the most important point the writer makes. The main idea tells what the whole paragraph is about. Often a writer provides the main idea in a clear topic sentence at the beginning or the end of a paragraph.
>
> ▶ **Details** are bits of information in sentences that support the main idea in a paragraph.

Identify

Find a paragraph in "Starting a Business" that has a clearly stated main idea. Write the page number and the main idea of the paragraph. Then list two sentences with details the writer gives to support the main idea.

1. Page: _____ Main Idea: _____

_____

_____

Detail: _____

_____

_____

Detail: _____

_____

_____

UNIT 2 Dollars and Sense • **Lesson 1** *Starting a Business*

Practice

Read the paragraph below. Underline the main idea. Then write two sentences with details that support the main idea.

Today we have vaccines for many different diseases. A vaccine is a special chemical substance that protects us against a certain disease. The substance is made of weak disease germs that cause the body to produce cells to fight off the disease. Recently scientists have developed vaccines for chicken pox and some types of flu.

Detail: _____

_____

Detail: _____

_____

Apply

Write a paragraph about an idea for starting a business. State your main idea in the first sentence. Then add sentences with details to support the main idea.

_____

_____

_____

_____

_____

_____

_____

Types of Sentences

There are different types of sentences that writers use to create variety in their writing.

Rule	Example
▶ A **simple sentence** has one simple or compound subject and one simple or compound predicate.	▶ Money allows people to buy goods and services.
▶ A simple sentence is also called an **independent clause.** Two or more independent clauses joined with a comma and a coordinating conjunction, such as *and, or,* or *but* form a **compound sentence.**	▶ People once used gold and cattle as money, **but** they were too heavy to carry.
▶ A **complex sentence** has one independent clause and one or more dependent clauses. A **dependent clause** has a subject and a verb but cannot stand alone as a sentence. A comma is placed between the dependent clause and the independent clause.	▶ Because it was also dangerous to carry a lot of gold, people began to use paper money.

Read the sentences. Identify each one as *simple,* compound, or *complex.* Write the answer in the blank.

1. North America's first paper money was issued in 1685. _____

2. Coins were hard to find, and paper was easier to use. _____

3. When the country started to use the money, banks issued it. _____

4. Today the U.S. government is in charge of issuing money. _____

UNIT 2 Dollars and Sense • **Lesson I** *Starting a Business*

▶**Types of Sentences**

Practice

Read this paragraph. Underline each compound sentence once. Underline each complex sentence twice.

In 2000, the U.S. Mint issued a new coin. It is called the Golden Dollar. This coin can be used instead of a dollar bill. The coin can pay a toll on a highway, or a person might use it to buy a drink from a vending machine. While the Golden Dollar is a new coin, it isn't the only new coin the U.S. Mint has ever created.

Proofread

Read this paragraph. Write the letter *S* over each simple sentence. Underline each compound sentence once. Underline each complex sentence twice.

Because there are so many countries in the world, money comes in many different sizes and colors. Travelers can sometimes become confused about how much things cost. Some European countries decided to start using the same kind of money. These countries wanted travelers to visit, but they didn't want people to be confused about money anymore. The money is called the *euro*.

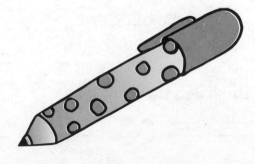

UNIT 2 Dollars and Sense • **Lesson I** *Starting a Business*

Sentence Combining

Combining sentences is one way to improve sentences that are short and choppy. Here are a few ways to combine sentences.

Rule	**Example**
▶ Combine two simple sentences by adding a conjunction to form a **compound sentence**.	▶ Practice is at 3:15. I don't want to be late. **Practice is at 3:15, and I don't want to be late.**
▶ Combine parts of sentences to form a new sentence with a **compound subject** or a **compound predicate**.	▶ Kelly asked for help. I asked for help. **Kelly and I** asked for help. Kelly raised her hand. Kelly asked for help. Kelly **raised her hand and asked for help.**
▶ Combine ideas to form a **complex sentence.** A complex sentence contains an independent clause and at least one dependent clause.	▶ My hair is wet. I forgot my umbrella. **My hair is wet because I forgot my umbrella.**

 **Combine each of these pairs of simple sentences to form compound sentences or sentences with compound parts.**

1. Jennie likes to skate. Maya likes to skate.

_____

2. We could play tennis. We could go swimming.

_____

3. Vince picked up the phone. He dialed the number.

_____

Practice

Read the following draft. Then improve it by combining sentences. Write your revision in the space provided.

My teacher fell on the ice. He broke his arm. It's his right arm. Mr. DeCarlo is left-handed. Sometimes he needs help. He needs help putting on his coat. He needs help carrying his briefcase. In one way, Mr. DeCarlo's broken arm has been a good lesson. We have learned to be sympathetic. We have learned to be helpful.

_____

_____

_____

_____

_____

_____

_____

_____

_____

_____

_____

_____

WRITER'S CRAFT

Capitalization

Capital letters are used in many places in writing.

Rule	**Example**
▶ Capitalize the first word in a sentence.	▶ **The boy bought a new skateboard.**
▶ Capitalize the name of a person, a place, or a thing.	▶ **Lyndon Johnson New York Eiffel Tower**
▶ Capitalize the title of a certain work, such as a book, a movie, a play, or a work of art.	▶ *Little Women* (book) *Fantasia* (movie) *Cats* (play) *Mona Lisa* (work of art)
▶ Capitalize the names of months, days, and holidays.	▶ **June Friday Mother's Day**

Read each sentence. If the words in bold type are capitalized correctly, write *yes* in the blank. If the words are not capitalized correctly, write *no* in the blank, then write the words correctly.

1. Do you like to cook **Mexican** food? _____

2. In **January,** Brian and his family will go skiing in

    Colorado. _____

3. My father and **jared** took a cab to the airport.

    _____

4. Molly went to her dancing class every **wednesday.**

    _____

5. The **chaneys** went to the restaurant after the game. _____

UNIT 2 Dollars and Sense • **Lesson 2** *Henry Wells and . . . William G. Fargo*

MECHANICS

Practice

Read each sentence. Cross out any word that is not correctly capitalized and write the correctly capitalized word above it.

6. egypt is a country in africa.

7. Many people have come from latin america and asia to live

   in the united states.

8. nicholas went to indianapolis, indiana, to watch the

   basketball tournament.

9. My sister will go to california in june to visit her friend

   from italy.

Proofread

Read this paragraph. Cross out any word that is not correctly capitalized and write the correctly capitalized word above it.

On saturday, tyler's parents took him to a chinese

restaurant for his birthday. uncle kenny and aunt susan came

all the way from new york to see tyler. They gave him a new

computer game called *amazing mazes 2000* and a book titled

scary stories for kids. tyler's little sister, caroline, wanted it

to be her birthday too, but her mother said she would have

to wait until april.

Organizing Expository Writing

When you write to give information or to explain something, you must organize the information for your readers. The method of organization usually depends on the type of information you are providing your readers. Three common methods are **compare and contrast, cause and effect,** and **question and answer.**

▶ You can **compare and contrast** two things to point out how they are alike and how they are different. This method works well for comparing two products, two characters in a book or movie, or two animals, for example.

▶ You can explore **cause-and-effect relationships.** Historians and scientists often use this method of organization. You might explain events that caused another larger event. You might explain what causes northern lights to appear in the sky.

▶ You can use a **question-and-answer approach.** Begin by asking a question. Then give the answer by explaining the process or providing background for the readers.

 **For each topic, tell whether the writer should organize the writing using compare and contrast, cause and effect, or question and answer.**

1. elementary school and middle school

_____

2. the benefits of participating in team athletic activities

_____

3. the impact of watching television after school

_____

UNIT 2 Dollars and Sense • **Lesson 2** *Henry Wells and . . . William G. Fargo*

▶ **Organizing Expository Writing**

Practice

Read each expository paragraph. After each paragraph, tell what method of organization the writer uses— compare and contrast, cause and effect, or question and answer.

4. Have you ever been tricked by nature? Some plants and animals are *supposed* to be tricky. For example, the walking stick looks like a stick so it doesn't get eaten. Chameleons change colors to fool their enemies, and some butterflies' wings have markings that look like owls. The markings scare away birds that might want to eat the butterfly.

_____

5. The team's old So-Hi shoes had great support. They were also sturdy and they lasted the whole season. Everyone on the team was satisfied with them. This season, the team is wearing Troopers. There have been two foot injuries already, and two players have had to replace shoes whose soles were damaged. Team members agree that So-Hi seem to be of better quality than Troopers.

_____

What after-school activities take place at your school? Are there athletic teams, art classes, or reading clubs available? Write a paragraph about one or several of these activities. Use compare and contrast, cause and effect, or question and answer to organize your paragraph.

_____

_____

_____

_____

Comprehension and Language Arts Skills

WRITER'S CRAFT

Periods and End Punctuation

Periods are used in many different ways in writing.

Rule	**Example**
▶ Use a period at the end of a declarative sentence and most imperative sentences.	▶ All jackets will be on sale on Friday. Give me the sunglasses on the table.
▶ Many abbreviations, titles of people, and street addresses also use periods.	▶ ounce—**oz.** Mister—**Mr.** apartment—**Apt.**
▶ **Acronyms and initialisms** are abbreviations that do **NOT** use periods.	▶ Federal Bureau of Investigation—**FBI** National Collegiate Athletic Association—**NCAA**
▶ Use a period when writing amounts of money or decimals.	▶ New houses built rose **25.2** percent last year. The tickets cost **$49.95** each.

There are two other types of end punctuation.

▶ A question mark is used at the end of an interrogative sentence.	▶ Where are you?
▶ An exclamation point is used at the end of exclamatory and some imperative sentences.	▶ I love this book! Stop the bus!

Try It!

Read each sentence. Put periods where they are needed.

1. John S Collins is running for mayor of the city.

2. Deliver the package to 215 Kensington Pkwy on Thursday.

3. The EPA is in charge of protecting the environment.

4. The sandwich cost $150.

5. Keisha received 955 out of 100 percent on the exam.

UNIT 2 Dollars and Sense • **Lesson 3** *Elias Sifuentes, Restaurateur*

▶ Periods and End Punctuation

Practice

Read this paragraph. Put periods, question marks, and exclamation points where they are needed.

Whose picture is on the $50 bill The answer to that question is Ulysses S Grant He was the 18th US President Did you also know that he was an officer in the US Army during the Civil War Fighting in a war sounds scary President Grant died eight years after he left office

Proofread

Read this paragraph. Put periods, question marks, and exclamation points where they are needed.

"This is going to be great" Stacy's uncle had gotten tickets to see the US play Russia in women's basketball The tickets had cost $2550, and Stacy had just bought a game program for $575 "Is it almost time for the game to start" Mrs Cooper, one of the people in charge of getting things ready for the game, told Stacy she wouldn't have to wait much longer By halftime, the US team had made 927 percent of their free throws Russia won the game by one point, but Stacy was still happy that she had gotten to see it

Comprehension and Language Arts Skills

MECHANICS

UNIT 2 Dollars and Sense • **Lesson 3** *Elias Sifuentes, Restaurateur*

Dialogue and Direct Speech

When characters in a story talk, their conversation is called **dialogue**. Dialogue is also a way to reveal details about characters. Good dialogue makes a story more interesting. **Direct speech** is like dialogue and is often used in expository writing.

Rule

▶ Each character's exact words are enclosed in quotation marks.

▶ Usually, a new paragraph begins each time the speaker changes.

▶ Punctuation for dialogue goes inside quotation marks.

▶ Speaker tags, such as *said Ben* and *Katie snapped*, must be used often enough for readers to keep track of who is speaking.

Example

▶ "I don't think Syd likes me anymore," Katie pouted. "She never hangs around after school. She goes dashing off with her sister and I never see her."

"Oh, Katie, didn't you know?" said Ben. "Syd's mom's been really sick. She just got out of the hospital."

"Well, why didn't she just tell me?" Katie snapped back, angry at being left out.

Read the passage below. Then answer the questions.

"That was so cool!" Lynn made one final twirl on her skates, then breathlessly flopped onto a park bench.

Jonas fell on the bench next to Lynn. "Never again!" he vowed. "Never! Never again!" He quickly unbuckled his skates.

"Aw, it's only your first time. It wasn't that bad," Lynn said with a laugh.

"Are you kidding?" Jonas moaned.

"I fell, too, remember? Want to go another lap?"

"Didn't you hear me? Never again!"

1. What do you learn about Jonas in the passage?

_____

Name _____ Date _____

▶ **Dialogue and Direct Speech**

Practice

**Rewrite each sentence or set of sentences as dialogue.
Capitalize, indent, and punctuate your dialogue correctly.**

2. I told Ron that I couldn't help him.

_____

_____

3. Ruth said we must have mushrooms on the pizza. Eric told
Ruth he is allergic to mushrooms.

_____

_____

_____

4. The lifeguard called to us that the dock was closed and we should get
off. We said we would.

_____

_____

_____

5. Julia asked Carlos to help hang her poster. He told her that
he would do it if he could find a ladder.

_____

_____

_____

WRITER'S CRAFT

Sequence

Focus Writers use signal words to help readers understand sequence. Sequence is the order of events in a story.

> Writers often use signal words called **time and order words** to show
> ▶ the passage of time in a story. Words such as *Tuesday, tomorrow*, and *the next day* show time.
> ▶ the order in which events take place. Words such as *first, then, so, when*, and *finally* show order.

Identify

Look through "Food from the 'Hood: A Garden of Hope." Find two sentences with time words and two sentences with order words. Underline the time and order words in each sentence.

1. Page: _____ Sentence with time words: _____

_____

_____

2. Page: _____ Sentence with time words: _____

_____

_____

3. Page: _____ Sentence with order words: _____

_____

_____

4. Page: _____ Sentence with order words: _____

_____

▶ **Sequence**

Practice

Underline the words that signal time or order in each sentence.

5. We planted a garden in the spring.

6. First, we turned over the soil and took out all the weeds.

7. Then, we planted the seeds and watered the soil.

8. When the seeds sprouted, we watched carefully for signs of insects and other garden pests.

9. We took care of the garden for three months.

Apply

Write a paragraph about some of the things you did yesterday. Use time and order words to indicate when and in what order you did each thing.

_____

_____

_____

_____

_____

_____

_____

_____

_____

_____

COMPREHENSION

Commas

Commas are used to separate groups of numbers, words, or ideas.

Rule	**Example**
▶ Use a comma to separate items in a series.	▶ Andrea does not like asparagus, peas, or squash.
▶ Use a comma to separate elements in an address.	▶ The President lives at 1600 Pennsylvania Avenue, Washington, D.C.
▶ A comma is used in direct address.	▶ Darren, would you please take out the trash?
▶ A comma is also used in dates.	▶ On July 20, 1969, Neil Armstong walked on the moon.
▶ Use a comma after an interjection or introductory words or phrases that begin a sentence.	▶ Yes, I would like some ice cream. After school, Janet will walk the dog.

Read each sentence. Place commas between the words in a series and to separate the names of places in a sentence.

1. Rock jazz country and classical are different types of music.

2. Duke Ellington Dizzy Gillespie and Ella Fitzgerald are three famous jazz musicians.

3. Many jazz songs come from African-American work songs spirituals and folk music.

4. Country music first became popular when people began to listen to a radio show in Nashville Tennessee.

Commas

Practice

Read this paragraph. Place commas where they are needed.

String woodwind brass and percussion instruments make up the four sections of an orchestra. Some sections like percussion and brass make sounds in different ways. A musician strikes a percussion instrument to produce sound but air must be blown into a brass instrument. When an orchestra performs it is important for the musicians to pay attention to the conductor.

Proofread

Read this paragraph. Place commas where they are needed.

Tamara are you ready to go to the ballet? Ballets are graceful flowing and often tell a story. Long ago ballet dancers used to entertain kings queens and their families. *Swan Lake* a very famous ballet was first danced in St. Petersburg Russia. It is a story about a prince a young woman and an evil magician. *The Nutcracker* is another famous ballet and it is performed at holiday time in December.

MECHANICS

UNIT 2 Dollars and Sense • **Lesson 4** *Food From the 'Hood: A Garden of Hope*

Compare and Contrast

Comparing and contrasting is one way to organize information in expository writing. It is sometimes useful to compare and contrast two items, such as two objects, two events, two ideas, or two people or characters. Comparing and contrasting details can help support the main idea in a piece of writing.

▶ When collecting or organizing information to compare and contrast, a Venn diagram is a good tool to use. Here's an example.

Cats and Dogs as Pets

Cats	Cats and Dogs	Dogs
• more independent • don't need to be walked	• fur needs grooming • daily food and water	• need a lot of attention • need to be walked

 **Create a Venn diagram to organize ideas for the following topic.**

Compare and contrast two types of flowers or trees.

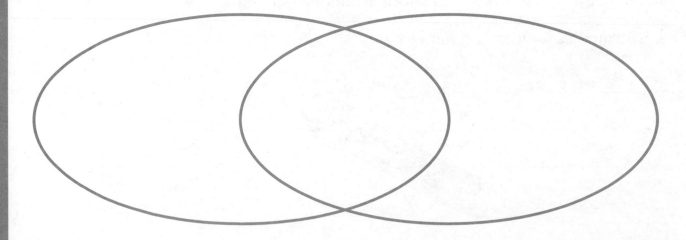

▶ Compare and Contrast

Practice

Look at each pair of words below. Write how the items in each pair are different and how they are alike.

1. book   computer

Different: _____

_____

Alike: _____

_____

2. babies   puppies

Different: _____

_____

Alike: _____

_____

Now choose one of the word pairs and compare and contrast the items in one or two paragraphs. Remember to vary your sentence structure so your writing is interesting.

_____

_____

_____

_____

_____

_____

_____

WRITER'S CRAFT

Quotation Marks and Underlining

Use quotation marks

Rule	**Example**
▶ to set off the exact words of a speaker in dialogue, or direct speech	▶ "Yeah," Leanne answered, "it's going to be a great party!"
▶ around a direct quote from another work or text	▶ Renaldo "knew Jinx was excited" when he told her about his idea.
▶ around the title of a poem or a short story	▶ "Hippopotamus" by Barbara Juster Esbensen
▶ If the speaker's words form a question, place the question mark *inside* the quotation marks. If the quotation does not form a question, the question mark is placed *outside* the quotation marks.	▶ "What time are you leaving to go to the party?" Leanne asked. Why does the invitation say, "Do not wear jeans"?
▶ Underline titles of works, such as books, movies, works of art, or music albums, if you are writing them by hand. If you type, use italics for titles.	▶ *Have you read the book* <u>Shiloh</u>? Da Vinci's *Mona Lisa* is in the Louvre in Paris.

Read this dialogue. Put quotation marks where needed.

Dominic and Kendra, please come here, Mom said. Have you taken Freckles out for her walk yet?

I did it last time, Dominic complained. It's Kendra's turn!

Says who? said Kendra. I always take Freckles on her walks!

Please stop arguing, Mom said. Why don't both of you walk Freckles?

I guess we'll both do it, sighed Kendra.

Quotation Marks and Underlining

Practice

Read each sentence. Underline the appropriate titles and put quotation marks where they are needed.

1. Gingerbread Days is the title of a book of poems by Joyce Carol Thomas.

2. February Hero, April Medicine, and Crawdads in July are titles of three of the poems.

3. A Gingered January is my favorite poem in the book.

4. Something BIG Has Been Here is a book of funny poetry by Jack Prelutsky.

5. The poem I Met a Rat of Culture has a lot of words in it that sound interesting.

6. I'll have to use my Webster's New World Dictionary to find out what these words mean.

Proofread

Read this dialogue. Underline any appropriate titles and put quotation marks where they are needed.

What movie are we going to see after the party? asked Leanne.

I don't know, said Lu. Does the movie Space Penguins from Pluto sound good to you? It's supposed to be really funny!

Leanne replied, Yeah, but my mom said I can't be out late. I have to finish the poem for my homework.

My poem's finished, said Lu, but I have to think of a title for it.

Maybe I'll write a poem about space penguins! Leanne chuckled.

MECHANICS

UNIT 2   Dollars and Sense • **Lesson 5** *Business Is Looking Up*

Developing Expository Writing

▶ Expository writing—writing that informs or explains—may require some special preparation. In many cases, a writer may need to conduct research before writing an expository piece.

▶ Once a writer chooses a topic and a main idea, she must decide how best to support that main idea. Will she use facts, reasons, and examples as support? It's important to think about what kind of information a main idea needs for support.

▶ In addition to gathering and analyzing information, a writer must also begin planning how to present it. Will the expository text be organized in time or sequential order, in order of importance, or in a compare-and-contrast format? The manner of presentation affects how the writer should organize her prewriting. For example, she might record her information on a time line, on a flow chart, or on a Venn diagram.

▶ Knowing what kind of information is needed, finding that information, and organizing it are all important steps to take as a writer develops a piece of expository writing.

 **Try It!** **Tell whether each of the following main ideas would most likely require facts, reasons, or examples as support for the main idea. Then explain your answer. The first item is done for you.**

1. Having a French class would work at our school because it works at other elementary schools.

   examples; Writer should give examples of other schools' successful French classes.

> **Developing Expository Writing**

WRITER'S CRAFT

2. Athletic programs in our school are growing each year.

_____

_____

3. Teenagers who take on part-time jobs hurt their grades.

_____

_____

4. Kids our age should cut down on time spent watching television.

_____

_____

Practice

Choose one of the topics in the Try It exercise, or think of another topic on your own. Jot down the facts, reasons, or examples you would need to write an expository piece on that topic. Then, write how you would organize the information.

Topic: _____

_____

_____

_____

_____

_____

_____

Colons, Semicolons, and Other Marks

Here are some punctuation marks you might use in your writing.

Rule	**Example**
▶ A colon is used to introduce a list of items.	▶ The main dishes that will be served at the wedding are these: prime rib, roasted chicken, and grilled fish.
▶ A colon is also used to show hours and minutes.	▶ The movie starts at 8:45 p.m.
▶ Use a semicolon in a compound sentence that does not have a coordinating conjunction. Place it between the two independent clauses.	▶ Kevin's class is performing a skit about the Civil War; his teacher picked him to play Abraham Lincoln.
▶ Use a hyphen in fractions that are spelled out and in some compound nouns.	▶ Add one-eighth of a teaspoon of salt to the recipe. Heather's self-esteem was high after she won the award.
▶ Use parentheses around words that add information to a sentence.	▶ Chocolate ice cream (my favorite flavor) can be found in almost any ice cream store.
▶ Use a dash to show that the thought in a sentence has been interrupted.	▶ Everyone—except me—already knows how to swim.

Read each sentence. Add colons, semicolons, and parentheses where they are needed.

1. The seven continents are listed here North America, South America, Europe, Asia, Africa, Australia, and Antarctica.

2. The Pacific Ocean which is 12,925 feet deep is the largest ocean on Earth.

UNIT 2 Dollars and Sense • **Lesson 6** *Salt*

► Colons, Semicolons, and Other Marks

Practice

Read each sentence. Add hyphens and dashes where they are needed.

3. Amanda was trying to make her great grandmother's famous cinnamon rolls for breakfast.

4. The secret ingredient that her great grandmother always added was one fourth teaspoon of honey.

5. Just as she was about to measure out the correct amount of honey, Amanda heard or thought she heard a noise outdoors.

6. Amanda accidentally dropped the open jar of honey, and she watched as a glob the size of a half dollar fell into the bowl.

7. Amanda knew there was too much honey in the bowl indeed there was but she baked the cinnamon rolls anyway.

Proofread

Read this paragraph. Add colons, commas, semicolons, hyphens, dashes, and parentheses where they are needed.

It was 1030 when Terry got out of bed. She looked at the long list of chores that her parents had left for her to do vacuum the living room and dining room, wash the dishes, water the plants, and finish her English project. She had been working on the project for a week all Terry had to do was write her final copy. Matt her step brother was at soccer practice, so she had the entire house to herself. Terry decided to watch TV for only a few minutes, but oh no she fell asleep again! Matt saw Terry asleep on the couch when he got home he woke her up and they finished the chores together.

MECHANICS

Plot

▶ A good story has a **plot** with a clear beginning, middle, and end. The **beginning** is where the problem is introduced. In the **middle,** the characters struggle with the problem and how to solve it. The events should build up to the exciting part where the characters solve the problem. The point at which the characters solve the problem is called the **climax.** After the problem is solved, the story ends.

 **Try It!** **Write the following events from a story in the order in which they would happen in the plot.**

▶ Grandmother hurts her leg in a fall and must ask Sharon for help.

▶ Sharon goes to her grandmother's house unwillingly, feeling unwanted by her parents.

▶ Sharon is told by her parents that she will spend the summer with her grandmother.

▶ Sharon finally feels wanted and needed by someone.

1. _____

_____

2. _____

_____

3. _____

_____

4. _____

_____

UNIT 2 Dollars and Sense • **Lesson 6** *Salt*

Practice

Think of a story or novel that you really enjoyed. In the space below, record the main events of the plot. Divide the events into the categories shown.

Title of story or novel: _____

Beginning: _____

_____

_____

Middle: _____

_____

_____

_____

Climax: _____

_____

_____

_____

Conclusion: _____

_____

_____

_____

_____

WRITER'S CRAFT

Review

▶ Types of Sentences

Identify each sentence as *simple*, *compound*, or *complex*.

1. Daily exercise helps keep the human body in shape.

_____

2. Because you're moving when you exercise, your heart pumps more blood throughout your body.

_____

3. Exercise gives you strong, flexible muscles, and it helps

you stay at a healthy weight. _____

▶ Capitalization

Cross out any word that is not correctly capitalized and write the word correctly capitalized above it.

4. The chinese new year falls somewhere between january 10 and february 19.

5. mr. rosen will celebrate a birthday in september.

6. i have to write a note to aunt elaine to thank her for the

trip we took to california and nevada in may.

▶ Periods and End Punctuation

Put periods, question marks, and exclamation points where they are needed.

7. Sen Hamilton made a donation to UNICEF

8. Wow Sasha won 962 percent of the votes in the election

UNIT 2 Dollars and Sense • **Lesson 7** *The Milkmaid and Her Pail*

Commas

Place commas where they are needed.

9. The tallest dams in the United States are in Colorado Arizona Idaho and Nevada.

10. Seoul South Korea; Barcelona Spain; and Sydney Australia have all hosted the Summer Olympic Games.

▶ Quotation Marks and Underlining

Underline any appropriate titles and put quotation marks where they are needed.

11. Dennis, what are you doing? Tanya asked her brother.

12. I'm reading Superfudge by Judy Blume. Have you heard of that book?

Colons, Semicolons, and Other Marks

Add colons, semicolons, hyphens, dashes, and parentheses where they are needed.

13. Totally Sports sells skates in four colors black, silver, navy blue, and red.

14. Carmen was so excited she could hardly wait to get to the store!

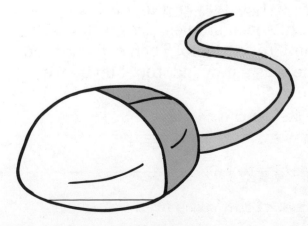

GRAMMAR, USAGE, AND MECHANICS

Supporting Details

▶A good paragraph has two elements. It has a main idea, stated in a topic sentence. The rest of the paragraph, then, consists of supporting details. Those details tell more about the main idea.

▶Supporting details might be reasons, examples, description, or facts. Different kinds of writing require different kinds of details. For example, a paragraph in a piece of persuasive writing might contain reasons.

▶In a story, a paragraph's main idea is likely to be supported by descriptive details. Descriptive details may also support the main ideas in an informative report or article. Facts are also likely to be important supporting details in a report or article.

▶The important thing about supporting details is that they tell more about the main idea of the paragraph. If they don't, they don't belong in that paragraph. Decide whether you should remove the detail completely or whether you should move the detail to a new paragraph.

 **Read the paragraph. In the space below, write the main idea and two supporting details in the paragraph.**

1.　I couldn't wait for the day to be over. No one spoke to me all day. At lunch, I fumbled my way through the hot lunch line, then ate alone. In social studies class, I thought for a minute a girl was going to say hello. Then she changed her mind. It turned out she was a new kid, too. Maybe we should start a club.

Main idea: _____

_____

Supporting Details

Practice

Provide at least two supporting details for each of the following topic sentences.

2. We could tell from the sky that we were really in for it.

_____

_____

_____

3. Many people don't realize that dolphins are mammals.

_____

_____

_____

4. Terry was my best friend, but I didn't know what to say.

_____

_____

_____

5. Chocolate is made from the beans of the cacao tree.

_____

_____

_____

WRITER'S CRAFT

Apostrophes

Apostrophes are used in contractions and possessive nouns.

Rule	**Example**
▶ In a **contraction,** an apostrophe takes the place of the missing letter or letters.	▶ they + are = they're would + not = wouldn't I + will = I'll
▶ To show possession, add an apostrophe plus **s** to a singular noun or a plural noun that does not end in **s**.	▶ Krista**'s** violin our library**'s** chairs the team**'s** coach the children**'s** room
▶ Add only an apostrophe after a plural noun that ends in **s**.	▶ the girls**'** laughter the dogs**'** owners

Read each sentence. Put apostrophes in each contraction.

1. The class hadnt visited Shedd Aquarium before.

2. "Its home to thousands of beautiful fish," the guide told the students.

3. "Please dont tap on the glass," she instructed.

4. "Thats very disturbing to the fish," the guide said.

5. At the Shedd, theres a giant squid hanging from the ceiling.

6. "Wouldnt it be neat if we were allowed to hang from the ceiling too?" asked one of the students.

7. The students couldnt see some of the fish in the aquariums because they had hidden so well.

UNIT 3 From Mystery to Medicine • **Lesson I** *Medicine: Past and Present*

▶ **Apostrophes**

Practice

Read each sentence. Put apostrophes in each possessive noun.

8. In some countries, a sharks fin can be made into soup.

9. Fire beetles eggs are often planted in smoldering trees.

10. The worlds fastest land animal is the cheetah, which can travel up to 70 miles per hour.

11. A human beings fastest running speed is still slower than many animals fastest speed.

12. A frogs skin is lighter in color than a toads skin.

13. The birds seeds and berries had disappeared, so they began to eat clay instead.

14. Scientists use a gorillas nose print to tell one gorilla from another.

Proofread

Read this paragraph. Put apostrophes where they are needed.

Arent sharks scary? Believe it or not, theyre probably more scared of us than we are of them. Sharks body parts are made into food and medicines. In some countries restaurants, shark fin soup is a very expensive dish. Shark hunters actions kill up to 70 million sharks every year. Many people say that this cant continue to happen. Female sharks dont have babies quickly, so the worlds sharks might be in trouble. To help preserve the shark, hunters must stop what theyre doing.

MECHANICS

UNIT 3 From Mystery to Medicine • **Lesson I** *Medicine: Past and Present*

Avoiding Wordiness

When writing is too wordy, it's not as effective as it might be. Good writers use only as many words as they need. They make every word count.

When you write, keep these points in mind:
▶ Use only as many words as you need to make your point.
▶ Choose simple, clear words or expressions, not complicated ones.
▶ Don't repeat words or ideas unless it is necessary to the meaning of your writing.

Here are some ways to avoid wordiness in your sentences.
▶ Remove groups of unnecessary words.
▶ Replace complicated or overly formal words with more simple ones.
▶ Shorten a clause to a phrase or even to a single word.

 **Each of the following sentences contains an unnecessary word or phrase. Rewrite each sentence, omitting the wordy part.**

1. In this novel, the alien space creatures are from Pluto.

_____

2. During the spring months is when I most enjoy the weather.

_____

3. Football players must wear protective equipment such as helmets, knee pads, and shoulder pads.

_____

4. We boarded a small boat that was floating on the surface of the lake.

_____

▶ **Avoiding Wordiness**

Practice

Some wordy clauses or phrases can be replaced by a shorter clause or phrase or by a single word. Rewrite each sentence. Replace the underlined clause or phrase with a more simple expression. In some sentences you may need to rearrange words.

5. In the event that I get my homework done, I can go to the game tonight.

   _____

6. That dance class that has been cancelled will be rescheduled.

   _____

7. I earned money by means of babysitting on Friday nights.

   _____

8. The kangaroo is a marsupial due to the fact that it has a pouch.

   _____

9. We agree that adding on to the house at this point in time is not a good idea.

   _____

10. In spite of the fact that it was cold and windy, our field trip was great.

   _____

WRITER'S CRAFT

Drawing Conclusions

Focus Writers provide information in a story to help readers draw conclusions about characters and story events.

> ▶ **Drawing conclusions** means taking small pieces of information about a character or story event and using them to make a statement about that character or event.
>
> ▶ The **conclusion** may not be stated in the text but should be supported by details in the text.

Identify

Look through "Sewed Up His Heart." Choose a character or a story event and draw a conclusion about it. Write the character's name or the story event. Then write your conclusion, two sentences from the story with details that support your conclusion, and the page numbers where the sentences are found.

Character or story event: _____

Page: _____ Sentence with details: _____

_____

_____

Page: _____ Sentence with details: _____

_____

_____

Conclusion: _____

_____

_____

► Drawing Conclusions

Practice

Read the paragraph and then draw a conclusion. Write the sentences from the paragraph that have details which support your conclusion.

The thin young woman stood as still as the flag that hung motionless in the summer air. Her head was bowed. The audience too was quiet. Suddenly she raised her head and paused, then ran at top speed. She leaped high into the air, clearing the high-jump bar. She jumped from the platform where she had landed, smiled widely, and raised her hands high above her head. The audience cheered and clapped wildly.

Conclusion: _____

_____

Detail: _____

_____

Detail: _____

_____

Apply

Write two sentences with details about a friend or member of your family. Then draw a conclusion about him or her from the details in the sentences. Write the conclusion in the space below.

Sentence: _____

_____

Sentence: _____

_____

Conclusion: _____

COMPREHENSION

Verb Tenses

Verb tenses show when an action takes place in a sentence.

Rule	**Example**
▶ A **present tense** verb shows the action is happening now. To form the present tense, add *-s* or *-es* to a regular verb that has a singular subject in a sentence. If the subject is plural, do not add *-s* or *-es* to the verb.	▶ The horse **jumps.** The horses **jump.**
▶ A **past tense** verb tells about action that has already taken place. To form the past tense of a regular verb with a singular or plural subject, add *-ed* to the verb.	▶ The horse **jumped.** The horses **jumped.**
▶ Some verbs don't follow rules for forming the past tense. **Irregular verbs** change their spelling for the past tense.	▶ The jockey **rides** the horse. (present tense) The jockey **rode** the horse. (past tense)
▶ The **future tense** tells about an action that will happen in the future. Use the helping verb *will* in front of the base form of a verb to show the future tense.	▶ The horse **will jump** over the water.

 **Try It!** **Read this paragraph. Change the underlined verbs from the present tense to the past tense. Write the correct word above the incorrect one.**

Alexander Fleming <u>live</u> from 1881 to 1955. He <u>discover</u>

penicillin. In a lab experiment, Dr. Fleming <u>have</u> bacteria

growing in a container. Some mold <u>get</u> into the experiment

by accident and <u>kill</u> the bacteria. This discovery <u>help</u> create

a brand-new medicine.

UNIT 3 From Mystery to Medicine • **Lesson 2** *Sewed Up His Heart*

▶**Verb Tenses**

GRAMMAR AND USAGE

Practice

Read the sentences. Change the words in parentheses to either the past tense or the future tense. Write the correct word above the word in parentheses.

1. Jorge (study) tomorrow for the science test.

2. Questions about seven famous scientists (be) on tomorrow's exam.

3. Damon and Duane (study) yesterday afternoon.

4. Later that evening, their mother (tell) them to go upstairs to wash up for supper.

5. Yesterday, Jorge (call) Damon and Duane to ask them some questions about the test.

6. After Jorge called, the two brothers (decide) to help Jorge.

7. All three boys think they (do) well on the test tomorrow.

Proofread

Read this paragraph. Change the underlined verbs to either the past tense or the future tense. Use proofreading marks to show changes. Write the correct word over the incorrect word.

Alexandra <u>is</u> sick yesterday. She <u>take</u> the science test

tomorrow. The rest of the class <u>take</u> it two days ago.

When I go to science class today, Mr. Crawford <u>tell</u> us

when he <u>give</u> us our tests back. I hope that it <u>be</u> soon.

The test <u>is</u> not that difficult for me, but I <u>study</u> for it for

two hours. I wonder how the other kids <u>do</u>?

Place and Location Words

A writer who organizes information in order must use place and location words to tell readers where things are or where actions take place. Here are some common place and location words:

about	*above*	*across*	*along*	*among*
around	*at*	*behind*	*beside*	*by*
down	*in*	*near*	*on*	*out*
over	*past*	*through*	*to*	*under*
up	*within*	*without*	*into*	*outside*

 **Try It!**   **Underline the place or location word in each sentence.**

1. Every few minutes, a train roars past.

2. The keys lay hidden inside her purse.

3. Celia passed the ball across the court.

4. Walking beside my dad always makes me feel short.

5. Mr. Griswald's store at the corner is for sale.

6. Our troop is picking up trash by the river.

7. Marcus looked down at the floor, scuffing his feet.

8. The tree went right through the roof.

UNIT 3 From Mystery to Medicine • **Lesson 2** *Sewed Up His Heart*

▶ **Place and Location Words**

Practice

Read each sentence starter. Then add a place or location word and any other words necessary to complete the sentence. A sample has been done for you.

We piled the groceries *on the counter.*

9. There was a window _____

10. The kite sailed _____

11. The clowns tumbled _____

12. The fire alarm startled everyone _____

13. My cousin goes to school _____

14. The kangaroo jumped _____

15. The playful puppy peeked _____

16. Paul's house is _____

Now describe one section of your school's lunchroom. Decide where you're going to start, then continue in an organized way, either left to right, right to left, top to bottom, or bottom to top. When your paragraph is complete, underline the place and location words you used.

_____

_____

_____

_____

_____

_____

WRITER'S CRAFT

Author's Point of View

Focus Every story is told from a specific point of view. Writers must decide on the point of view from which a story is told.

Authors create a narrator through which their stories are told. The narrator is the person telling the story. The narrator can tell the story from

▶ the **third-person point of view.** The narrator is not a character in the story and uses pronouns such as *he, she,* and *they* when telling about the characters.

▶ the **first-person point of view.** The narrator is a character in the story and uses pronouns such as *I, me,* and *my* when telling the story.

Identify

Look through the first two pages of "The Bridge Dancers." Find a sentence that lets you know what point of view the author chose for the story. Write the page number, the sentence, and the point of view. Then answer the question below.

Page: _____

Sentence: _____

_____

Point of view: _____

Why do you think the author chose this point of view?

_____

_____

_____

▶**Author's Point of View**

Practice

Read each paragraph and fill in the point of view.

1. Mary had never eaten a cucumber in her whole life. When she saw that her plate was full of cucumber slices, she almost gave it back. Then she decided to be brave and eat this new vegetable.

   Point of view: _____

2. Damian got a trampoline on his birthday. I got a pair of socks. Everything seems to go right for Damian, but nothing ever goes right for me.

   Point of view: _____

3. The garden was full of weeds. It would take hours to pull out all the weeds. Gina promised to take care of the garden, but she was visiting her grandfather. There was no one around to pull the weeds—except me. So I knelt down and got to work.

   Point of view: _____

Apply

Rewrite one of the passages above using a different point of view.

_____

_____

_____

_____

_____

_____

COMPREHENSION

UNIT 3 From Mystery to Medicine • **Lesson 3** *The Bridge Dancers*

Subject-Verb Agreement

Subject-verb agreement in a sentence means the verb agrees with the subject in number.

Rule	**Example**
▶ The subject of a sentence is either singular or plural. When a singular or plural noun or pronoun is the subject of a sentence, the verb must agree with the subject in number.	▶ **Petra** works at the movie theater. She **works** at the movie theater. We **work** at the movie theater.
▶ A **compound subject** that uses the conjunction *and* takes a verb that agrees with a plural subject. However, in a compound subject that uses or, the verb must agree with the *closest* subject word.	▶ Justin and Kayla **swim** for the Hillsboro Aquasharks. Their sisters or their brother **cooks** dinner for them every night.
▶ In a sentence with a singular subject, add -*s* or -*es* to a regular verb. In a sentence with a plural subject, do not add -*s* or -*es* to the verb.	▶ Raul **eats** lunch at the diner. The teenagers **eat** lunch at the diner.
▶ Irregular verbs have plural forms that are quite different from their singular forms. Do not add -*s* or -*es* to these verbs to make the plural forms.	▶ Mrs. Kent **has** an appointment. Her daughters **have** a band concert.

 **Read the paragraph. Circle the verb in parentheses that agrees with the subject of each sentence.**

How (do, does) people (decide, decides) what to watch on TV? Sometimes, they (take, takes) turns or (flip, flips) a coin. Parents often (tell, tells) their children which programs (is, are) appropriate. Parents (want, wants) to make sure the television programs they choose (is, are) good for kids to watch.

Practice

Read the sentences. Change the underlined verbs to agree with the subject of each sentence. Write the correct words above the underlined words.

1. Fossils <u>is</u> the remains of animals and plants that <u>has</u> died.

2. Fossils <u>forms</u> from objects that <u>is</u> hard.

3. Some fossils <u>looks</u> like dinosaur footprints.

4. A scientist <u>need</u> a microscope when the fossils <u>is</u> very small.

5. A piece of amber <u>trap</u> an insect and <u>create</u> a fossil.

Proofread

Read the paragraph. Change the underlined verbs to agree with the subject of each sentence. Use proofreading marks. Write the correct words above the incorrect words.

Roxie and Madison <u>takes</u> swimming lessons every week.

They <u>rides</u> their bikes to the community center after school.

Madison <u>enjoy</u> swimming the butterfly, but Roxie <u>hate</u> that

stroke! The girls' parents or their sisters <u>gives</u> them rides

home after practice. Roxie's brother and her dog <u>is</u> scared of

water. They both <u>screams</u> if water <u>touch</u> them. A dog treat or

a pat on the head <u>are</u> a way to quiet the dog. A bowl of

chocolate pudding <u>do</u> the trick for Roxie's brother.

Figurative Language

A figure of speech is a word or group of words that stands for more than its literal meaning. Writers use figures of speech, or **figurative language,** to help create pictures in readers' minds. There are different types of figurative language, including simile, metaphor, personification, and exaggeration.

Rule	**Example**
▶ A **simile** compares two things that are not alike by using the word *like* or *as*. In a simile, one thing is said to be *like* another.	▶ The lake looked like a mirror.
▶ A **metaphor** also compares two things that are not alike. A metaphor does *not* use *like* or *as*. In a metaphor, one thing is said to *be* another.	▶ The lake was a mirror.
▶ **Personification** is giving human qualities to objects, plants, or animals.	▶ Our cat lay on the floor, thinking hard about where the mouse might be. The fried eggs stared up at me, daring me to eat them.
▶ **Exaggeration** is a writer's way of stretching the truth to add humor or interest to details in a story, such as a tall tale, or another type of writing.	▶ Our cat was so big that people mistook her for a tiger.

 **Try It!** **Identify each of the following as an example of simile, metaphor, personification, or exaggeration.**

1. _____ The boards groaned under the weight of the workers.

2. _____ Her hands were machines that worked the knitting needles without even thinking.

3. _____ Mr. Riley's office was so messy you couldn't tell if he was in there or not.

▶ **Figurative Language**

Practice

Follow the direction to create your own figurative language.

4. Compare a river with a snake. Use a simile.

_____

_____

5. Compare a plate of spaghetti with a mountain. Use a metaphor.

_____

_____

6. Write another metaphor that includes either spaghetti or a mountain.

_____

_____

7. Use personification to describe rush-hour traffic in a big city.

_____

_____

8. Personify something in your classroom.

_____

_____

9. Use exaggeration to describe today's weather.

_____

_____

WRITER'S CRAFT

Fact and Opinion

Focus Writers use facts and opinions to support ideas in their writing.

> ▶ A **fact** is a statement that can be proven true.
> ▶ An **opinion** is what someone feels or believes is true. Opinions cannot be proven true or false.

Identify

Look through "Emily's Hand-On Science Experiment" for examples of facts and opinions. Write two facts and two opinions on the lines below.

1. Page: _____

Opinion: _____

_____

2. Page: _____

Fact: _____

_____

3. Page: _____

Opinion: _____

_____

4. Page: _____

Fact: _____

_____

▶ **Fact and Opinion**

Practice

Read the sentences below. Write *fact* if the sentence is a fact or *opinion* if it is an opinion in the spaces below.

5. _____ All German shepherd dogs are mammals.

6. _____ The success of a business depends on the age of its owners.

7. _____ Chicago is a city in the state of Illinois.

8. _____ The *Titanic* was a large ship that sank in the Atlantic Ocean.

9. _____ Being on salary is better than taking a percentage of the income.

Apply

Write two sentences that are facts and two sentences that are opinions about the town or city in which you live.

10. _____

_____

11. _____

_____

12. _____

_____

13. _____

_____

COMPREHENSION

Pronoun-Antecedent Agreement

A **pronoun** takes the place of one or more nouns.

Rule	**Example**
▶ The noun to which a pronoun refers is called the **antecedent.** A pronoun's antecedent usually comes *before* the pronoun. The pronoun must agree with its antecedent in number. This is called **pronoun-antecedent agreement.**	▶ Dustin picked up the **books** and put **them** on the table.
▶ An antecedent may also be in a previous sentence.	▶ Alicia saw the new **bikes** at the store. **They** were blue and gold.
▶ A compound subject is considered one antecedent.	▶ **Pete and I** ran to class. **We** didn't want to be late.

 **Try It!**

Read the paragraph. Use the pronouns *they, them,* **and** *it* **to correct the underlined pronouns. Write the correct word above the incorrect word.**

The United States has fifty-five national parks. <u>It</u> can be found in many states. The Everglades is a national park in Florida. <u>They</u> was established in 1934, and <u>they</u> is home to rare birds and alligators. Alligators have sharp teeth, but <u>it</u> aren't as fierce as crocodiles.

Pronoun-Antecedent Agreement

GRAMMAR AND USAGE

Practice

Read the paragraph. Circle the correct pronoun in each set of parentheses.

Jessica's family is going on vacation. (He, They) will be gone for two weeks. Jessica is so excited to leave that (she, we) has been packing for three days. "(We, I) am so happy that (we, I) are going to see the Grand Canyon," Jessica said with a smile. "(They, It) looks so big!" Jessica is getting impatient as (she, us) waits. "Aren't (it, we) ready to go yet?" she asks. Finally, (they, she) are all ready to leave.

Proofread

Read the paragraph. Look at each underlined pronoun. Change each incorrect singular pronoun to the correct plural pronoun. Change each incorrect plural pronoun to the correct singular pronoun. Use proofreading marks and write the correct word above the incorrect one. Write *correct* if the pronoun is correctly used.

"My family and I weren't the only people to visit the Grand

Canyon," Jessica said. "Over three million visitors come to see

they each year. My parents, my brother, and us walked along

the South Rim three times. She were tired when she were

finished. Some people wanted us to go with her to the North

Rim, but she went back to our hotel."

Tone of a Personal Letter

> ▶ The tone of a piece of writing is the feeling the writer conveys. A writer's tone may be serious or funny, light or sad. A writer's tone is affected by the words he chooses and how he expresses himself.
>
> ▶ In a personal letter, the tone should be friendly. After all, it's not a business letter. A good way to think of a personal letter is a one-way conversation with a friend. The writing may sound a lot like a conversation you would have with a classmate or a brother or sister.
>
> ▶ In informal writing, the sentences may be short, like the ones we use in everyday conversation. Sentences may include contractions, abbreviations, and perhaps even slang. In general, the words are simple, not complicated.

Try It! **Make an X in front of each sentence that has a friendly tone and might be used in a personal letter.**

1. _____ Have you heard about our new puppy?

2. _____ I sure had a good time at your house last weekend.

3. _____ I am writing to ask for information from your company.

4. _____ Carl, Megan, and I wish to thank you for the present you sent.

5. _____ I hope soccer practice has been going well.

6. _____ Last week we took a field trip to a greenhouse.

Tone of a Personal Letter

Practice

Follow the instructions to practice creating a tone that is right for a personal letter. Imagine that you are speaking with or writing to a friend or relative as you practice. For each item, write two sentences.

7. Write about the trouble your new pet has caused. Use a funny tone.

    _____

    _____

8. Tell someone who has been sick that you hope he or she can come back to school soon. Use a serious but friendly tone.

    _____

    _____

9. Use a funny tone to tell about how nice or how awful the weather has been.

    _____

    _____

10. Thank someone for a card or gift, using a friendly tone.

    _____

    _____

    _____

WRITER'S CRAFT

Making Inferences

Focus Readers make inferences about characters and events to understand the total picture in a story.

An inference is a statement about a character or event in a story. To make an inference, the reader uses
▶ **information** from the story, such as examples, facts, reasons, and descriptions.
▶ **personal experience or knowledge,** which is the individual memories and experiences you bring to the story.

Identify

Look through "The New Doctor." Choose a character or a story event and make an inference about it. Write the character's name or story event in the spaces below. Then write the information from the story, the page number, and personal experience or knowledge and make an inference.

Character or story event: _____

_____

Page: _____ Information from the text: _____

_____

_____

_____

Personal experience or knowledge: _____

_____

Inference: _____

_____

Making Inferences

Practice

Read the paragraph and make an inference. In the spaces below, write the inference and the information and personal experience or knowledge you used to make the inference.

At home, Jeanette takes care of all her family's pets. She also walks two big dogs for Mrs. Yamamoto, her next-door neighbor. In addition to these tasks, Jeanette helps her cousin Lila herd sheep for a farmer. She doesn't yell at the sheep to make them go into the corral the way Lila does. Instead, Jeanette gently pushes them into the corral.

Inference: _____

Information from the paragraph: _____

_____

Personal experience or knowledge: _____

_____

Apply

Write a short paragraph about Manuelita in "The New Doctor." Use sentences with information that a reader could use to make an inference about her. Use a separate sheet of paper if you need more space.

_____

_____

_____

_____

_____

_____

COMPREHENSION

UNIT 3 From Mystery to Medicine • **Lesson 5** *The New Doctor*

Intensive, Reflexive, and Demonstrative Pronouns

Intensive, reflexive, and demonstrative pronouns express different things about a noun in a sentence.

Rule	**Example**
▶ An **intensive pronoun** draws attention to a noun or pronoun in the same sentence.	▶ The twins cleaned up their room by **themselves.**
▶ A **reflexive pronoun** refers to the subject of a sentence and receives the action of the verb.	▶ Angela told **herself** not to be afraid on the roller coaster.

Both intensive and reflexive pronouns end with *-self* or *-selves.*

▶ A **demonstrative pronoun** points out a particular person, place, or thing. *This* and *these* refer to people, places, or things that are nearby. *That* and *those* usually refer to people, places, or things that are farther away.	▶ **This** is a workbook page about grammar. **These** are the books. **That** was the best lunch ever! **Those** were delicious sandwiches.

Read the paragraph. Circle the correct demonstrative pronoun in each set of parentheses.

Today, I ate two muffins. (These, Those) were the muffins on the table in the middle of the kitchen. (This, That) was the first time I had ever eaten a cranberry or pecan muffin. Because I had never eaten any like (these, those), I wasn't sure I would like them. I was glad I didn't have to worry about (this, that), because the muffins tasted great!

UNIT 3 From Mystery to Medicine • **Lesson 5** *The New Doctor*

Intensive, Reflexive, and Demonstrative Pronouns

Practice

Fill in the blank with an intensive or reflexive pronoun.

1. Trevor, Lynn's little brother, often says, "I can do it

   _____!"

2. "You will have to make dinner for _____
   tonight because I have a meeting," Mom said.

3. Lynn couldn't solve the math problem _____,
   so she asked Mom before the bus came.

4. "Mom will let us go to the mall by _____ on
   Saturday," Lynn told Mark.

5. "The noise will stop by _____ if you are
   patient," Mom said.

6. "Remember, Trevor can feed _____ if you cut
   up his food for him."

7. "Tell Mark and Trevor to clean the living room by

   _____."

Proofread

**Read the conversation. Circle the correct pronoun in
each set of parentheses.**

"Is (this, that) the report that Claire wrote by (myself,
herself)?" Mrs. Lynch asked Kristen, as she held up Claire's
paper.

"Yes," Kristen said. "(This, That) is Claire's report. I wrote
mine by (itself, myself), and Claire wrote hers by (herself,
yourself)."

Mrs. Lynch opened the report and showed Kristen one
page. "Did Claire tell you where she got the pictures?"

GRAMMAR AND USAGE

Aim, Purpose, and Audience

Before a writer begins any writing project, it is important to know exactly what his aim, purpose, and audience are.

▶ A writer's aim is the message he wants to convey. The aim is closely tied to the writer's purpose for writing. For example, the aim of a writer who publishes an informative article about killer whales might be to share knowledge. His aim also may be to raise readers' awareness of threats to the whales' existence. So he is doing more than just *informing* his readers, even though that is his basic purpose.

▶ A writer's purpose may be to inform, to explain, to entertain, or to persuade. Sometimes a writer may have more than one purpose. For example, a writer may use humor to persuade his readers about something. His purpose, then, would be to entertain *and* to persuade.

▶ The audience is the people who will read or hear the written product. It's important to know who the audience is as you write. For example, if you are writing for grown-ups, you may use different words or a different tone than if you are writing for your classmates.

 **Identify the purpose of each topic below—to inform, to explain, to entertain, or to persuade.**

1. _____ trying new things—and enjoying it

2. _____ ads and how they affect our buying habits

3. _____ the power of showing respect for others

4. _____ why school should start at 8:15

UNIT 3   **From Mystery to Medicine • Lesson 5** *The New Doctor*

▶ Aim, Purpose, and Audience

Practice

Tell what kind of audience each of these products might be written for. Be as specific as you can.

5. an illustrated version of a fairy tale

_____

6. a scientific report about a new medicine

_____

7. an article about diamonds in a magazine titled *Young Discoverer*

_____

8. a letter of complaint about a spoiled food product

_____

9. an article about keeping fit in a magazine titled *Senior Life*

_____

10. an editorial in a local newspaper about the mayor

_____

Now practice writing for different audiences. First write a note to one of your parents about your day. Then write a journal entry (that you are willing to share) about how your day went.

Dear _____ ,   Dear Journal,

_____   _____

_____   _____

_____   _____

_____   _____

WRITER'S CRAFT

Cause and Effect

Focus Cause-and-effect relationships help readers understand why events happen in a certain way.

> ▶ A **cause** is why something happens.
> ▶ The **effect** is what happens as a result.
> ▶ Writers use signal words and phrases to identify cause-and-effect relationships. These words, which include *because, so, if, then, thus, since, for,* and *therefore,* help readers know what happens and why it happens.

Identify

Based on what you read in "The Story of Susan La Flesche Picotte," fill in the spaces below with the cause or effect that completes the sentences.

1. When Susan got the reservation physician position, she did

not receive more money because _____

_____

_____ .

2. Because many of the houses were getting old and had not

been kept in repair, _____

_____

_____ .

3. If Susan's horse Pie hadn't stopped over Jimmy, _____

_____

_____ .

▶**Cause and Effect**

Practice

Rewrite each pair of sentences as one sentence showing the cause-and-effect relationship.

4. My mother is going to be late. I am cooking dinner.

_____

_____

5. Isabel loves to read. She got a library card.

_____

_____

6. I worked hard on my paper. I will get a good grade.

_____

_____

7. Adam will be late. Start without him.

_____

_____

Apply

Think about a game you played in or watched recently. Write a short paragraph describing the action in the game, using words and sentences that show a cause-and-effect relationship.

_____

_____

_____

_____

COMPREHENSION

Adjectives and Adverbs

Adjectives and adverbs modify other words in a sentence.

Rule	**Example**
▶ An **adjective** is a word that describes a noun or a pronoun.	▶ **red** sweater **blue** moon
▶ A **proper adjective** describes a noun and begins with a capital letter.	▶ **Chinese** food **French** bread
▶ *A*, *an*, and *the* are special adjectives called **articles.** *The* refers to a particular person, place, or thing. It is called a **definite article.** The words *a* and *an* are **indefinite articles.** They refer to any one person, place, or thing.	▶ **The** milk is cold. Almost every city has **a** zoo.
▶ A **demonstrative pronoun** can also be used as an adjective to point out a particular person, place, or thing.	▶ **These** boats sailed across the ocean.
▶ An **adverb** is a word that describes a verb, another adverb, or an adjective.	▶ She walked **quickly.**

Sometimes *bad, badly, good,* and *well* are used incorrectly.

▶ *Bad* is used as an adjective, and *badly* is used as an adverb.	▶ This is a **bad** apple. Emma sprained her ankle **badly.**
▶ *Good* is used as an adjective, and *well* is used as an adverb.	▶ That is a **good** explanation. Antonio did **well** on the test.

Read the conversation. Circle the articles and underline the other adjectives in the paragraphs below.

"Do you want me to buy a new book for you to read?" Dad asked Valerie.

"Yes," Valerie said. "The one I want is about aquatic life in the Atlantic Ocean. It has a blue cover and beautiful pictures taken by the diver with an underwater camera. I would like to take underwater pictures when I'm older. Do you think it's a good idea?"

Practice

Read the paragraph. Underline the adjectives and circle the adverbs in the sentences.

Ian is an Australian athlete. He is tall and strong. Ian swims well during his races, and he is a good sport whether he wins or loses. His coach often tells him to behave politely to others when he doesn't win a race. Ian had one difficult race. A Dutch swimmer was able to beat Ian easily. Ian remembered what his coach told him. He was the first person to tell the winner that he did well.

Proofread

Read the paragraph. Circle the correct adjective or adverb in each set of parentheses.

Have you ever been to (the, an) (italian, Italian) restaurant in Italy? (A, The) menu that you are given has (Italian, italian) words in it, but sometimes (the, a) waiter or waitress at your table is able to tell you the (English, english) meaning of the words. People in Italy love (good, well) food, but they think that cold drinks can hurt your stomach (bad, badly), so they don't use a lot of ice.

Time and Order Words

Time words and phrases tell when things happen. Here are some common time expressions:

today	*after class*	*in the morning*	*next week*
Friday	*one month*	*last summer*	*a year ago*

Order words tell in what order events happen. Order words help readers understand steps in an experiment, events in a story, or a series of historical events. Here are some common words that signal time order:

after	*before*	*finally*	*first*	*last*	*later*
meanwhile	*next*	*second*	*then*	*third*	*until*

Notice how the time and order words in this paragraph make the order of events clear.

Example

It's hard to believe that it was only <u>last summer</u> that we got Rags. I can still see him curled up in a tiny ball in his basket. <u>Then</u> he outgrew his basket. <u>After that,</u> he used the basket for a chew toy. In <u>December</u> he moved out to his doghouse. <u>Now</u> he weighs 75 pounds. And <u>next week</u> he'll be one year old.

Read each sentence. Write the words that tell time or order in the space provided.

1. It was only after lunch that we learned the truth.

_____

2. The meeting is next Tuesday.

_____

3. Next brush the glue onto Parts D and E.

_____

4. Kay and Satsuki met at noon at the library.

_____

Practice

Improve each sentence or passage by adding time or order words or phrases. In some cases you will be adding interest. In some cases you will be making the order of events more clear.

5. We got out the ice cream. We scooped the ice cream into our cones.

_____

6. I must have lost my homework. (Hint: Tell when this happened.)

_____

7. The awful battle took place. The wounded soldiers had to wait to get help.

_____

8. The sea looked green. It looked pinkish. It got dark.

_____

9. Cut several lengths of string. Attach the strings to a clothes hanger. Attach the plastic fish to the strings. Hang up your mobile.

_____

_____

WRITER'S CRAFT

Review

▶ Apostrophes

Read each sentence. Place apostrophes where they are needed.

1. Didnt Mom tell Patrick to change out of his dress clothes after Aunt Karens wedding?

2. Devons favorite meal was not on the menu, so he couldnt order it for dinner.

▶ Verb Tenses

Read each sentence. Circle the correct verb tense in each set of parentheses.

3. Our class (went, will go) to the science museum next Friday.

4. Jamal (choose, chose) Troy to be his partner on the trip.

5. We (were, are) excited about tomorrow's trip to the new dinosaur exhibit.

▶ Subject-Verb Agreement

Read each sentence. Circle the correct form of the verb in each set of parentheses.

6. Tammy (has, have) a dance recital this afternoon.

7. Her mother (tell, tells) Tammy that her costume isn't ready yet.

8. Tammy (reminds, remind) her that they must (leaves, leave) soon.

► **Review**

► Pronoun-Antecedent Agreement

Read each sentence. Circle the correct pronoun in each set of parentheses.

9. Greg hopes (he, them) can visit his cousin this summer.

10. Brian and Greg have started to plan what (he, they) want to do during their vacation.

► Intensive, Reflexive, and Demonstrative Pronouns

Read each sentence. Circle the correct pronoun in each set of parentheses.

11. "Didn't Dad say that you'll have to pay for the new model by (yourself, yourselves)?" asked Audrey.

12. "Yeah," said Ned. "Look! (These, Those) models over there are the ones on sale!"

13. "Ned, if I loan you some money, we can buy an expensive model by (ourselves, himself)."

► Adjectives and Adverbs

Read each sentence. Circle the correct adjective or adverb in each set of parentheses.

14. (A, The) man I'm talking about wore a (Scottish, scottish) kilt, and he played his instrument very (well, good).

15. He didn't play a single note (bad, badly), and he gave everyone (a, the) smile when people asked him questions.

GRAMMAR, USAGE, AND MECHANICS

Aim, Purpose, and Audience

Before a writer begins any writing project, it is important to know exactly what his aim, purpose, and audience are.

▶ A writer's aim is the message he wants to convey. The aim is closely tied to the writer's purpose for writing. For example, the aim of a writer who publishes an informative article may be to raise readers' awareness of an issue. So he is doing more than just *informing* his readers, even though that is his basic purpose for writing.

▶ A writer's purpose may be to inform, to explain, to entertain, or to persuade. Sometimes a writer may have more than one purpose. For example, a writer may choose to use humor while explaining a process. His purpose, then, would be to explain *and* to entertain.

▶ The audience is the people who will read or hear the written product. It's important to know who the audience is as you write. For example, if you are writing for grown-ups, you may use different words or a different tone than if you are writing for your classmates.

 **Try It!**   **Identify the purpose of each topic below—to inform, to explain, to entertain, or to persuade.**

1. _____ benefits of exercise

2. _____ how to enjoy being a bench warmer

3. _____ our school uniforms should be updated

4. _____ kachina dolls

5. _____ the process of photosynthesis

6. _____ how to make a potato clock

►**Aim, Purpose, and Audience**

Practice

Tell what kind of audience each of these products might be written for. Be as specific as you can.

7. a letter requesting donations for a local charity

_____

8. a scientific report about a new earthquake-proof building method

_____

9. an article about New Orleans in a Minnesota newspaper

_____

10. a story, with pictures, about an ant and a cricket

_____

11. a report about health care reform

_____

12. an editorial in a newspaper about a local law

_____

Now practice writing for different audiences. First, write a note to a grown-up in which you explain a career path that interests you. Then, write a brief report for your classmates about that same career path. Make sure you use an appropriate tone in each writing product.

Dear _____ , | Career Report

_____ | _____

_____ | _____

_____ | _____

_____ | _____

_____ | _____

WRITER'S CRAFT

UNIT 4 Survival • **Lesson I** *Island of the Blue Dolphins*

Comparative and Superlative Adjectives

Rule	**Example**
▶ Use the comparative form to compare two things. For one-syllable adjectives, add -*er* to form the comparative.	▶ Tran is **taller** than her sister is.
▶ Add *more* to most adjectives with two or more syllables. Do **not** add -*er* to the end of the adjective.	▶ The puzzle was **more challenging** than Lisa thought it would be.
▶ To compare three or more things, use the **superlative** form. Superlative forms of most one-syllable adjectives end in -*est*.	▶ Tran is the **tallest** girl in her family.
▶ Add *most* to most adjectives with two or more syllables to form their superlatives.	▶ The puzzle was the **most challenging** one that Lisa had ever put together.
▶ Some adjectives, such as *good*, *bad*, and *many*, have different comparative and superlative forms.	▶ Her grandmother's soup is **good.** Her grandmother's soup is **better** than yours is. Her grandmother's soup is the **best** in the town.

 **Try It!** **Read the sentences. Circle the correct comparative or superlative adjective in parentheses.**

1. Which amusement park is (biggest, bigger), Splash City or World of Fun?

2. World of Fun has the (scarier, scariest) roller coaster that I've ever ridden.

3. The (more dangerous, most dangerous) thing to do on a roller coaster is not to fasten your harness properly.

Comparative and Superlative Adjectives

Practice

Read the sentences. Write the comparative or superlative form of the adjective in parentheses in the blank.

4. Today is the _____ day Tina has had all week. (bad)

5. She got up late, so her brother got _____ cereal than Tina did. (many)

6. Tina likes her green sweater _____ than her blue one, but her green sweater wasn't clean. (good)

7. Her score on her math quiz was _____ than the score she got last week. (bad)

8. She will have to spend _____ time on her math than she did before. (many)

Proofread

Read the paragraph. Cross out any of the underlined comparative or superlative adjectives that are incorrect. Write the correct adjective over the incorrect one. Use proofreading marks to show the corrections.

Jon's baseball card collection is the <u>bigger</u> collection in

town. He even has <u>most</u> cards than the new sports store that

opened last month. Jon is <u>carefuler</u> with his baseball cards

than he is with any other thing that he owns. The <u>more</u>

<u>expensive</u> card in his collection comes from the 1920s. Jon

says that the <u>bad</u> thing to do to a baseball card is to bend it.

GRAMMAR AND USAGE

UNIT 4 Survival • **Lesson I** *Island of the Blue Dolphins*

Organization of a Narrative Paragraph

A **paragraph** is a group of related sentences that support one main idea. Each paragraph introduces a new idea. The first sentence is indented. In some forms of writing, such as narrative, a paragraph can be one sentence.

A **topic sentence** tells the main idea of the paragraph. Other sentences in the paragraph give details that support the topic sentence. Be sure that every sentence in the paragraph relates to the topic sentence.

The supporting sentences can be arranged in **order of time** or **order of impression.**

Rule	**Example**
▶**Order of time** tells *when* or in what *order* things happen. Use order of time to inform or instruct the reader.	▶If you want to learn to play golf, lessons are a good first step. *First* you will learn the correct way to hold the club. *Next* you will learn how to stand. *Then* you will learn all about how to hit the ball.
▶**Order of impression** organizes the details from most important to least important. You must decide what matters the most to you.	▶I can't wait to go on our school field trip to the science museum. I love wandering through the giant maze, getting lost and bumping into dead ends. I also like the machine that feels like we are riding in space.

UNIT 4 Survival • **Lesson I** *Island of the Blue Dolphins*

Organization of a Narrative Paragraph

Try It! **Read each of the paragraphs and follow the instructions below.**

1. Underline the topic sentence in this paragraph.

   Thunderstorms can cause a lot of damage. Too much rain can cause flooding. Lightning can strike objects, causing them to fall or catch on fire. Strong winds can blow things around or knock down trees. Some thunderstorms have hail that can dent cars and break windows. Thunderstorms can even produce tornadoes.

2. Underline the topic sentence in this paragraph, then cross out any sentences that do not support the main idea.

   Our science teacher has asked us to draw pictures of the moon. I wonder how old the moon is. She wants us to look for and sketch the light and dark colored areas. She will display our work on the bulletin board. Later we will make clay models from our drawings.

Practice

Write a paragraph organized by order of impression or order of time. You could write about your favorite cousin, why you like ice cream, your favorite animal, the things your mother does that drive you crazy, or some other topic. Be sure you have a topic sentence and that all your other sentences relate to the topic sentence.

_____

_____

_____

_____

WRITER'S CRAFT

UNIT 4 Survival • **Lesson 2** *Arctic Explorer: The Story of Matthew Henson*

Comparative and Superlative Adverbs

Rule	**Example**
▶ Use the **comparative** form of an adverb when comparing two verbs. Add *-er* to compare with most one-syllable adverbs.	▶ Beth can swim **faster** than Kimberly.
▶ Use *more* with most adverbs that have two or more syllables to form the comparative.	▶ Some people can type **more quickly** than they can write.
▶ When comparing three or more verbs, use the **superlative** form. Add *-est* to most one-syllable adverbs to make the superlative form.	▶ Beth swims the butterfly the **fastest** of any of her teammates.
▶ Use *most* with most adverbs with two or more syllables to form the superlative.	▶ Sean is the one who can type the **most skillfully** in our group.
▶ Some adverbs, such as *well, badly, much,* and *little,* have different comparative and superlative forms.	▶ Tia plays video games **better** than her brother does. However, her brother talks **more** than she does.

 **Read the sentences. Circle the correct comparative or superlative form of the adverb in parentheses.**

1. Will was the person in our group waiting (more patiently, most patiently) for his sandwich.

2. Dad also reminded Will and Randy that they had to run (most carefully, more carefully) in the sack race than they did last year.

3. Tara said she'd rather see which frog could jump (higher, highest) in the frog-jumping contest.

UNIT 4 Survival • **Lesson 2** *Arctic Explorer: The Story of Matthew Henson*

Comparative and Superlative Adverbs

Practice

Read the sentences. Write the comparative or superlative form of the adverb in parentheses in the blank.

1. Connie, Leslie, and Heather write stories _____ than I do. (well)

2. Leslie uses her computer _____ than she uses paper and pencil. (much)

3. Of the four of us, Heather writes the _____. (little)

4. Leslie describes scenes the _____ out of anyone in our writing group. (well)

5. I write fantasy scenes _____ than any of my friends. (badly)

6. Leslie says worrying _____ might help me. (little)

Proofread

Read the paragraph. Cross out and correct any of the underlined comparative or superlative adverbs that are incorrect. Write the correct adverb over the incorrect one. Use proofreading marks to show the corrections.

Box turtles live <u>more long</u> than any other animal on our

planet. Opossums live an average of one year in the wild.

Polar bears usually do not live <u>longer</u> than humans, but they

can swim in cold water <u>easilyer</u> than a human can.

GRAMMAR AND USAGE

Suspense and Surprise

Using **suspense** and **surprise** helps make a story scarier, funnier, or more interesting.

Suspense is a feeling of uncertainty or anxiety about what might happen in a story. The readers keep reading because they want to know, "What's going to happen next?"

Here are some ways to build suspense.

Rule	**Example**
▶ Add sounds.	▶ The wind <u>howled</u>, and a dog <u>yipped</u> nervously in response.
▶ Use strong action verbs.	▶ Suddenly, a pole <u>crashed</u> to the ground.
▶ Use vivid adjectives.	▶ A <u>short, broad-shouldered</u> man in <u>dark</u> clothing leaned against the trunk of a <u>massive</u> oak tree.

Surprise is the readers' strong reaction to unexpected or unpredictable events. Their reaction is "I never expected that to happen!"

Here are some ways to create surprise:

Rule	**Example**
▶ Include unexpected events	▶ A police car pulled up to the house the broad-shouldered man had entered. Soon an officer led him out to the street.
▶ Add plot twists	▶ "Arrest him," the broad-shouldered man said, pointing at the man in the car. "That's my car. He stole it."

 **Try It!** In each sentence circle the word in parentheses that creates more suspense or surprise.

1. The wind (*blew, howled*).

UNIT 4   Survival • **Lesson 2** *Arctic Explorer: The Story of Matthew Henson*

▶ Suspense and Surprise

2. The rain (*battered, hit*) the window pane.

3. The man was so (*upset, shocked*) his hands shook and his heart pounded.

4. The magician (*said, mumbled*) a spell and, in a blink, the lion (*was gone, vanished*).

Practice

For each underlined word or phrase, write a word that creates suspense or surprise. (You can use words that change the meaning but create a suspenseful feeling.) Explain how your new word makes the sentence more interesting. The first one is completed for you.

5. "Go away," the woman said. *Begged. It shows she wasn't in control of the situation.*

6. The man was <u>standing</u> in the corner of the room.

_____

_____

7. The man <u>went</u> down the hill. _____

_____

8. The monster in the closet <u>scared</u> the little boy.

_____

_____

9. The <u>large</u> owl spread its wings and cast a <u>large</u> shadow

over the lawn. _____

_____

WRITER'S CRAFT

Author's Purpose

Focus Writers have reasons for presenting a story in a certain way.

> The **author's purpose** is the main reason for presenting a story or selection in a certain way. An author's purpose
> ▶ can be to *inform*, to *explain*, to *entertain*, or to *persuade*.
> ▶ affects things in the story, such as the *details*, *descriptions*, *story events*, and *dialogue*.
> An author can have more than one purpose for writing.

Identify

Look through "McBroom and the Big Wind." Identify the author's purpose for writing the story. Find two sentences with story events about the wind that show the author's purpose. Write the page numbers and the sentences. Then answer the questions below.

Page: _____ Sentence: _____

_____

_____

Page: _____ Sentence: _____

_____

_____

What is the author's purpose in this story? How successful

was the author in achieving his purpose? _____

_____

_____

Name _____ Date _____

▶ **Author's Purpose**

Practice

Read the title of each story below. Then write what the author's purpose might be for writing the story—to *inform*, to *explain*, to *entertain*, or to *persuade*.

1. *The Dog That Ate New York*

Author's purpose: _____

2. *Water Safety for Swimming-Pool Owners*

Author's purpose: _____

3. *The Care and Feeding of Mice*

Author's purpose: _____

4. *Why You Should Vote*

Author's purpose: _____

5. *My Mother, the Time Traveler*

Author's purpose: _____

Apply

Write a paragraph about McBroom and the wind to persuade readers that McBroom's story is true. Use a separate sheet of paper if you need more space.

_____

_____

_____

_____

_____

COMPREHENSION

UNIT 4 Survival • **Lesson 3** *McBroom and the Big Wind*

Conjunctions and Interjections

Rule

▶ A **conjunction** is a word that connects words or groups of words. The words *and*, *but*, and *or* are **coordinating conjunctions.** They connect related groups of words.

▶ **Subordinating conjunctions** introduce subordinate clauses. A subordinate clause is a part of a complex sentence that does not express a complete thought.

▶ An **interjection** is a word or group of words that expresses strong feelings. Interjections that express very strong emotions are followed by an exclamation point. A comma follows interjections that are not as strong.

Example

▶ You can either mow the grass **or** help me wash the car. Alex can help you, **but** she has other chores to do too.

▶ **Before** you leave, tell me what time you will be home. **Since** Mrs. Ruiz is driving you to practice, don't forget to thank her.

▶ **Oh no!** I forgot all about Sam's birthday!
Darn, I'll have to give him his present tomorrow.

 **Try It!**

Read the paragraph. Circle all of the coordinating conjunctions. Underline all of the subordinating conjunctions.

It is important to do some research before you decide to buy a pet. Pets may look cuddly and cute, but taking care of an animal is a big responsibility. Since pets can't tell their owners what they want or need by using words, humans must keep a close eye on them. Some people believe that cats are the easiest pets to keep. Others prefer smaller pets, like gerbils, hamsters, and fish. Whatever type of pet you choose, be sure that you are able to give it lots of love, care, and attention.

UNIT 4 Survival • **Lesson 3** *McBroom and the Big Wind*

Conjunctions and Interjections

Practice

Read the sentences. Add an exclamation point or a comma after each interjection.

1. Hey don't forget that it's your turn to take Ralph to the vet today.

2. No way I have a meeting at 3:30 p.m.

3. Sorry I forgot about your meeting.

4. Oh no I can't take him either because I have to teach a class at the university.

5. Oh well I guess I can be a few minutes late for the meeting.

6. Ralph Quit slobbering all over today's newspaper!

Proofread

Read the paragraph. Add conjunctions where needed to complete the sentences. Add an exclamation point or a comma after each interjection. Use proofreading marks for the corrections.

"Hey" Pat was angry, she couldn't help laughing at her dog. Diva had tried to run out the door and into the street, she had gotten all tangled up in her leash instead. She always started to bark she saw a car. She was afraid she'd miss something new exciting. "Hey, Diva you know it's not safe to run into the street," Pat said to the dog. They had gotten back into the house safely, the two of them sat on the couch Diva curled up into a little ball fell asleep.

GRAMMAR AND USAGE

Exaggeration

Exaggeration is a way of stretching the truth to add humor or interest to your writing. Exaggeration takes a statement or an opinion to an extreme that cannot be true. Exaggeration is often used in stories, such as tall tales, to create humor. Exaggerations are often statements of comparison *(more than, bigger than, as big as)*.

▶ **Rule**

Exaggerations are statements that stretch the truth.

▶ A *literal statement* (a statement of fact) is the opposite of an exaggerated statement. In a literal statement, the words mean what they say.

▶ **Example**

My brother is the best skier that ever lived in the whole history of the world.
▶ The living room in our new house is as big as the Sahara Desert.
▶ My brother is a good skier.
▶ The living room in our new house is really big.

In most writing, you don't want to use exaggeration too often; it will lose its humor and effectiveness.

Try It! Label each sentence with an *L* for literal or an *E* for exaggeration.

_____ 1. The fish that got away was about 12 inches long.

_____ 2. The concert was very crowded.

_____ 3. The tree was growing so fast, I would hear the bark stretching.

_____ 4. "The music is so loud, I think my head will explode," she said.

_____ 5. He ate enough to feed an army.

UNIT 4 Survival • **Lesson 3** *McBroom and the Big Wind*

▶ **Exaggeration**

Practice

Write an exaggerated statement for each of the sentences. The first one is completed for you.

6. I was really cold.

I was so cold my nose froze and fell off.

7. The man's voice was too loud.

_____

8. The birds are eating a lot of birdseed this winter.

_____

9. The fish that got away was huge.

_____

10. I am afraid of spiders.

_____

11. This hot chocolate is too hot to drink.

_____

12. The Olympic swimmer set a new speed record.

_____

13. We just bought a huge television set.

_____

14. Our dog is really funny-looking.

_____

WRITER'S CRAFT

UNIT 4 Survival • **Lesson 4** *The Big Wave*

Prepositions

Rule	Example
▶ A **preposition** is a word that relates a noun, pronoun, or group of words to some other word in the sentence. Prepositions usually indicate relationships of time or place.	▶ The cookies are **on** the third shelf. They are stacked **above** the crackers.
▶ The noun or pronoun that follows a preposition in a sentence is called the **object of the preposition.** A preposition must have an object. It can't stand alone.	▶ The box of spaghetti is **beneath** the **crackers.** (*Crackers* is the object of the preposition *beneath.*) The sauce should be **beside** the **spaghetti.** (*Spaghetti* is the object of the preposition *beside.*)
▶ A **prepositional phrase** is made up of a preposition, its object, and any words in between.	▶ The food is **in the cabinet.** The cabinet is **near the window.**

Try It!

Read the paragraph. Circle all of the prepositions.

   Mongolia is a country on the continent of Asia. It is above China and below Russia. The capital city is near a river. Ulan Bator, the capital city, is one of the largest cities in Mongolia. There are several large cities throughout China and Russia. Have you ever traveled around China and Russia?

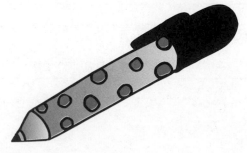

GRAMMAR AND USAGE

▶ **Prepositions**

Practice

Read the paragraph. Circle all of the prepositions. Write the word *object* above the object of the preposition.

Many people travel across North America in cars. The United States is between Canada and Mexico. The Rio Grande River runs along the American border with Mexico, but people can still drive to that country. Several of the Great Lakes are also near our border with Canada, but visitors can drive across them by using a bridge. Families sometimes visit Canada or Mexico during a vacation.

Proofread

Read the paragraph. Circle all of the prepositions. Draw an X through each object of a preposition. Underline each prepositional phrase.

People live in many different areas throughout the United States. Some live with animals on a farm. Others may live in an apartment in a big city. Another group might live near the water, and many children live on quiet streets in small towns. Considering the laws of our country, Americans can choose where they want to live.

UNIT 4 Survival • **Lesson 4** *The Big Wave*

Characterization

Characterization is the way to make a character come alive for your readers. *Show* how the character acts, thinks, feels, and speaks. Show how other characters respond to him or her.

Rule	Example
▶ Show how the character acts.	▶ Edward ran next door to his friend's house. He rang the doorbell over and over and over again.
▶ Show how the character thinks.	▶ He couldn't wait to show Luis his new skateboard. He knew Luis would be jealous.
▶ Show how the character speaks.	▶ When Luis came to the door, Edward bragged loudly, "What do you think? It was the most expensive skateboard in the entire mall. None of the other kids can afford this one."
▶ Show how the character feels.	▶ Luis didn't answer. But Edward just kept on talking as if he didn't even care what Luis thought.
▶ Show how other characters respond.	▶ "Edward is so selfish," Luis said to his mother later. "But someone has to be his friend."

Showing what characters are like is better than simply telling what they are like. You will make the characters seem like real people.

Try It! **Based on the example sentences in the box above, how would you describe Edward?**

_____

_____

Practice

Write a short characterization. You could write more about Luis (Edward's friend from the example on page 142) or you could write about another imaginary person, or someone you know. Make the person come alive for your reader.

_____

_____

_____

_____

_____

_____

_____

_____

_____

_____

_____

_____

_____

_____

_____

UNIT 4   Survival • **Lesson 5** *Anne Frank: The Diary of a Young Girl*

Author's Point of View

Focus   Every story is told from a specific point of view. Writers must decide on the point of view from which a story is told.

All stories are told through a narrator, which is the person who tells the story. The narrator can tell the story from

▶ the **third-person point of view.** The narrator is an outside observer and uses pronouns such as *he, she,* and *they* when telling the story.

▶ the **first-person point of view.** The narrator is a character in the story and uses pronouns such as *I, me,* and *my* when telling the story.

Identify

Look through "Anne Frank: The Diary of a Young Girl." Find three sentences that show the author's point of view. Write the page number, the sentence, and the point of view in the spaces below.

1. Page: _____   Point of View: _____

Sentence: _____

_____

_____

2. Page: _____   Point of View: _____

Sentence: _____

_____

_____

► **Author's Point of View**

Practice

Read the passage below. Answer the questions about the author's point of view.

My brother and I are building a doll house for our little sister. We have spent a lot of time building it, but I know it will be worth it. I'm so glad my brother knows how to measure and build things and wants to help me. He even helped me sew curtains for the windows! Our sister is going to love her birthday present from us.

3. What is the author's point of view? _____

4. What words tell you the author's point of view? _____

_____

Apply

Rewrite the above passage using the third-person point of view.

_____

_____

_____

_____

_____

_____

_____

COMPREHENSION

Double Negatives and Contractions

Rule	Example
▶ In English, we use only one negative word in a sentence. When two negatives occur in a sentence, we say the sentence contains a **double negative.**	▶ **Double Negative:** She **doesn't** have **no** homework to do tonight. **Corrected Sentence:** She **doesn't** have any homework to do tonight.
▶ A **contraction** is a shortened form of two words. The contractions *they're,* *you're,* and *it's* are the shortened forms of the words *they are, you are,* and *it is.* They are often confused with the possessive pronouns *their, your,* and *its. They're* is also sometimes mistaken for the word *there.*	▶ **They're** members of the new band I told you about. (This contraction is the shortened form of the two words *they* and *are.*) I've wanted to go to **their** concert for six months! (This possessive pronoun shows that this band is the one performing the concert.)

 **Read the sentences. Correct the double negatives and make words into contractions where they are needed.**

1. Tyrone says that there is not no one who will help him finish painting the house.

   _____

   _____

2. Jake will not help no one because it is going to get hot outside.

   _____

   _____

UNIT 4 Survival • **Lesson 5** *Anne Frank: Diary of a Young Girl*

Double Negatives and Contractions

Practice

Read the sentences. Circle the correct word in parentheses.

3. What time does (you're, your) brother's plane land?

4. His friends said (their, they're) going to pick him up at the airport at 2:00 p.m.

5. Since (its, it's) almost 1:30 p.m., they should leave soon.

6. Didn't you tell me that he's bringing his guitar and all of (it's, its) equipment with him?

7. (You're, Your) going to have a famous musician visiting you!

8. No, I'm not. (Its, It's) just my brother.

9. I'm going to watch the band and (their, they're) workers get ready for the concert.

Proofread

Read the paragraph. Cross out and correct any double negatives and any of the underlined words that are incorrect. Use proofreading marks for the corrections.

Nobody is going to buy none of <u>you're</u> candy bars. <u>There</u> the ones with coconut in them, and no one wants nothing to do with coconut! I know <u>its</u> not something that I like to eat. <u>You're</u> going to try and sell them to <u>you're</u> grandparents and <u>they're</u> friends, aren't you?

GRAMMAR AND USAGE

UNIT 4 Survival • **Lesson 5** *Anne Frank: Diary of a Young Girl*

Point of View

Point of view answers the question, "Who is telling the story?" Use the same point of view throughout the whole story so readers do not become confused.

The narrator (the storyteller) can tell the story from a **third person point of view** or a **first-person point of view**.

Rule

▶ **Third-person point of view**
The narrator is an outside observer and is not part of the action of the story. She uses pronouns such as *he, she, his, her,* and *they* when telling the story. The narrator may also tell the thoughts and feelings of one or more characters.

▶ **First-person point of view**
The narrator is a character in the story and uses pronouns such as *I, me, my, our* or *us* when telling the story. The story tells the thoughts and feelings of one character— the narrator.

Example

▶ The king rode silently through the forest. *(An outside observer is reporting actions.)*
▶ Neither <u>he</u> nor <u>his</u> knights sensed any danger. *(The outside observer is reporting feelings of the king and knights.)*

▶ <u>I</u> rode through the forest with the king. *(Narrator is a participant reporting her own actions.)*
▶ <u>I</u> didn't sense that <u>we</u> were in any danger. *(Narrator reports her own thoughts or opinions.)*

 **Identify the point of view in each sentence.**

1. Randy played with his friend Scott every day at recess and after school.

_____

2. I just didn't want to pretend to my mother I was happy.

_____

UNIT 4 Survival • **Lesson 5** *Anne Frank: Diary of a Young Girl*

▶ **Point of View**

Practice

Read the following passage. Answer the questions about the author's point of view.

Ralph and I wanted to go on an adventure. We wanted to go hiking on the Appalachian Trail this summer. My parents thought our idea was a good one, and they planned a family trip around our adventure!

1. What is the author's point of view? _____

2. What words tell you the author's point of view?

_____

Rewrite the paragraph above using the third-person point of view.

_____

_____

_____

_____

_____

_____

_____

_____

_____

WRITER'S CRAFT

Main Idea and Details

Focus Writers use a main idea and details to make their point clear in a paragraph.

> ▶ The **main idea** is the most important point the writer makes. The main idea tells what the whole paragraph is about. Often a writer provides the main idea in a clear topic sentence at the beginning or the end of a paragraph.
>
> ▶ **Details** are bits of information in sentences that support the main idea in a paragraph.

Identify

Find a paragraph in "Music and Slavery" that has a clearly stated main idea. Write the page number and the main idea of the paragraph. Then list two sentences with details the writer gives to support the main idea.

Page: _____

Main Idea: _____

_____

_____

Detail: _____

_____

_____

Detail: _____

_____

_____

UNIT 4 Survival • **Lesson 6** *Music and Slavery*

▶ **Review**

GRAMMAR AND USAGE

▶ **Prepositions**

Read the paragraph. Circle all of the prepositions. Draw an X through each object of a preposition. Underline each prepositional phrase.

Since we are going to the library, we should return the overdue books that are under your bed. One of my books is on the table by the window. Be sure to look around your room and see if there are any other books hiding in your closet. I found one leaning against the wall last week. We'll drive by the sandwich shop on our way to the library. Let's stop for lunch first.

▶ **Double Negatives and Contractions**

Read the paragraph. Correct any double negatives. Change the spelling of the underlined words or shorten them to contractions. Use proofreading marks for the corrections.

The library <u>does not</u> have no books about movie monsters, but the librarian said that <u>their</u> will be a new shipment of books coming next week. She told me that nobody has never asked her for a book about movie monsters before. If you've found <u>you're</u> book, you can go sit over <u>they're</u> and read it. I <u>do not</u> want to go home yet, do you? I know <u>its</u> time to go home and finish the dishes, but I still <u>have not</u> found no books yet.

Mood

> **Mood** is the tone or atmosphere of the story. Mood is often described with a feeling word. The mood could be happy, sad, angry, suspenseful, mysterious, exciting, and so on.
>
> Writers create mood through these story details:
>
> ▶ *Story events.* What kinds of things keep happening? Parties? Adventures? People disappearing? Unexpected events?
>
> ▶ *Setting* Where does the story take place? Brightly lit rooms? Forest? Meadow? A long hallway at the end of a rabbit hole? A palace?
>
> ▶ *Descriptions.* What colors are used—bright or dark? What are the sounds—happy birds chirping or rumbling thunder? What are the shapes and smells?
>
> ▶ *Choice of words.* Is the writer using humor? Exaggeration? Similes or metaphors that make silly or scary comparisons?
>
> ▶ *Character's emotions and reactions to events.* What are the characters feeling about the events or about the other characters?
>
> ▶ *Dialogue.* What do the characters say and how do they say it? Do they order or beg? Shout or whisper?

 **Identify the mood of the following paragraph and write the words or events that helped you identify it.**

Angela was tired and wanted to get home. She decided to take the shortcut her older sister had showed her. The woods were peaceful and calm. The trees stood tall, as if they would protect her. The bushes along the narrow path gently brushed her skin. Birds chirped high above her. Angela forgot she was tired.

_____

_____

UNIT 4 Survival • **Lesson 6** *Music and Slavery*

▶ Mood

Practice

Identify the mood of the sentence. Then change the underlined word(s) in each sentence to create the new mood that is listed.

...htened mouse, <u>afraid of becoming lunch</u>, looked at ...nd <u>fled</u> across the kitchen floor.

Rewrite:

_____

_____

2. The <u>red-faced</u> boy <u>angrily spit out</u> the words, "<u>You can't tell me to leave!</u>"

Mood: _____

New Mood: Sadness

Rewrite: _____

_____

_____

UNIT 5 Communication • **Lesson I** *Messages by the Mile*

Classifying and Categorizing

Focus Good readers classify items into categories as they read to help them organize information and understand what they read.

Classifying means arranging people, animals, or things into different groups or **categories.** When classifying people, ideas, places, or things

▶ name the categories, or groups, for similar items.
▶ list items that fit the category.

Animals ◀── *Category*
Bats
Lizards
Mice
Fish
Turtles

Some items can fit more than one category.

Animals	**Reptiles**
Turtles	Turtles
Lizards	Lizards

Identify

Look through "Messages by the Mile" and list all the items that fit the categories below.

1. Mammals: _____

_____

2. Mammals that live in water: _____

_____

3. Mammals that use infrasonic communication: _____

_____

UNIT 5 Communication • **Lesson I** *Messages by the Mile*

▶ Classifying and Categorizing

COMPREHENSION

Practice

Look at the items in the box below. List each item from the box under the correct category. Remember that some items can fit into more than one category.

Items			
notebook	fruit	juice	sandwich
stamps	paper	pen	

Things for Lunch	**School Supplies**	**Things for Writing and Mailing Letters**
_____	_____	_____
_____	_____	_____
_____	_____	_____

Apply

Whales have characteristics that make them different from other types of sea creatures. For instance, whales are mammals. Think of other types of animals, such as reptiles or birds. Name and write this new category for a type of animal. Then, list any animals that fit this category in the spaces below.

_____

_____

_____

_____

_____

UNIT 5 Communication • **Lesson I** *Messages by the Mile*

Phrases

Rule	**Example**
▶ A **phrase** is a group of words used as a single part of speech. A phrase may contain a verb, but it does not contain the verb's subject. Three kinds of phrases are *participial phrases*, *prepositional phrases*, and *appositive phrases*.	▶ **Splattered by mud**, Kisha's new coat looked brown instead of blue.
▶ A **participial phrase** functions as an adjective and includes a participle and other words that complete its meaning.	▶ **Walking home**, Kisha wondered what her mom would say.
▶ A **prepositional phrase** functions as an adverb or an adjective. A prepositional phrase begins with a preposition and always ends with the noun or pronoun.	▶ Mom put Kisha's coat **in a plastic bag.**
▶ An **appositive phrase** usually follows the noun it describes.	▶ The coat, **a gift from Kisha's cousin**, needed to be dry-cleaned.

 **Try It!** Read the following sentences and underline the participial phrase in each.

1. Cluttered by magazines and newspapers, the table was not a very clean place to work.

2. Looking at us carefully, Claire said, "Are you sure you want to sit here?"

3. Reaching for her chair, she sat down slowly.

Practice

Read the sentences. Underline the prepositional phrases. Circle the appositive phrases.

1. "According to Mrs. Cartwright, this project isn't due for two weeks, Morgan," I said.

2. Morgan, Claire's twin sister, always likes to get projects done early.

3. Mrs. Cartwright, the nicest teacher in our school, also told us that she'd give us time to work on our projects during class.

4. "Mrs. Cartwright gave us thirty pages to read for the project," Morgan reminded me.

5. Claire, a person who liked to study, had an idea about our conversation.

6. "Why don't we work on the project for an hour and then walk across the street to the movies?"

Proofread

Read the paragraph. Draw a box or square around the participial phrases. Underline the prepositional phrases. Circle the appositive phrases.

We worked on the project until 4:30. Morgan, one of the fastest readers in the fourth grade, was happy because we were able to read fifteen pages of information. Yawning because I was bored, I begged her, "Can we please go to the movies now?" Claire, the world's biggest popcorn fan, agreed with me. She couldn't wait to get to the theater. I stood behind Morgan and took the pencil out of her hand. "Let's go," I said. "We're leaving."

Developing Persuasive Writing

The purpose of persuasive writing is to convince your readers to believe, think, feel, or act a certain way. Here are two ways to persuade your readers.

▶ One way is to support your opinion with *facts and reasons*. You might need to do research to find facts to back up your opinion.

▶ Another way to persuade your readers is to appeal to their *interests* or *emotions*. You would need to understand your readers and figure out what they care about.

Whether you choose facts or feelings to persuade readers may depend on who your audience is. Will your audience respond better to facts or feelings?

There are different techniques you can use to organize the facts or emotional appeals in your persuasive writing. One way is to ask questions and give answers. Asking a question is a good way to grab a reader's attention.

Example

Why is toothpaste with fluoride good to use? For one reason, a toothpaste with fluoride helps keep teeth strong and healthy.

For each persuasive topic below, choose the most effective approach—facts or feelings—and briefly explain why.

1. A note to persuade your parents to take you to Disney World.

_____

2. A letter to the editor of the newspaper calling for better school lunches.

_____

3. A school newspaper ad for a candy sale fundraiser.

_____

UNIT 5 Communication • **Lesson I** *Messages by the Mile*

Practice

Choose one of the topics from page 160 listed below and write a question and possible answers that you might use in a persuasive piece. Keep in mind the type of appeal you are making—fact or feeling—as you write your question and answers.

4. A note to persuade your parents to take you to Disney World.

Question: _____

_____

Possible Answers: _____

_____

_____

5. A school newspaper ad for a candy sale fundraiser.

Question: _____

_____

Possible Answers: _____

_____

_____

Choose one of the topics above and write an introductory paragraph. Use your question and answers to develop your paragraphs.

_____

_____

_____

WRITER'S CRAFT

Developing Persuasive Writing

Fact and Opinion

Focus Writers use facts and opinions to support ideas in their writing.

> ▶ A **fact** is a statement that can be proven true.
> ▶ An **opinion** is what someone feels or believes is true. Opinions cannot be proven true or false.

Identify

Look at the statement about "We'll Be Right Back After These Messages." In the spaces next to each statement, write *fact* if the statement is a fact. Write *opinion* if it is an opinion.

_____ 1. An average television viewer watches 20,000 commercials in a year.

_____ 2. Seeing a baseball player advertise a bat or ball will make you want to buy one.

_____ 3. Being able to see bands perform their songs on TV makes people more likely to buy their records and concert tickets.

_____ 4. The FCC has hundreds of rules governing the television industry.

_____ 5. The advertising industry in Canada and the United States must obey special rules for advertising to children under 12.

_____ 6. Music videos can use the same techniques as in regular commercials to get and hold your attention.

_____ 7. When an American music video channel started showing videos in 1981, music sales boomed.

_____ 8. You can watch an ad on TV without even knowing it's an ad.

▶ **Fact and Opinion**

Practice

Add a fact or an opinion to each sentence below. Use the clues in parentheses.

9. (opinion) Cats like to _____

_____

10. (fact) All books have _____

_____

11. (fact) Some birds are _____

_____

12. (opinion) All children are _____

_____

Apply

Think about how advertising techniques are used to get your attention. Based on what you learned from "We'll Be Right Back After These Messages," write two sentences about ads that are facts and two that are opinions.

13. _____

_____

14. _____

_____

15. _____

_____

16. _____

_____

COMPREHENSION

▶ Clauses

Rule	**Example**
▶ An **adjective clause** is a dependent clause that works the same way as an adjective. An adjective clause tells *how many, what kind,* or *which one* about the noun or pronoun it modifies.	▶ The house **where Diedre's grandparents lived** was built before the Civil War.
▶ An **adverb clause** is a dependent clause that acts as an adverb. Like an adverb, an adverb clause modifies a verb, an adjective, or another adverb. They tell *where, when, why, how,* or *to what degree.* Adverb clauses are always introduced by subordinating conjunctions.	▶ Diedre has visited her grandparents every summer **since she was three years old.**

**Read the sentences. Underline the
adjective clause in each sentence.**

1. Mike was the new kid whose family had moved into the house on the corner.

2. We watched the movers carry boxes that had stamps from other countries on them.

3. We guessed the boxes that had the letter "M" on them belonged to Mike.

4. Mike's mom was the woman whom my mother had spoken to on the phone last week.

UNIT 5 Communication • **Lesson 2** *We'll Be Right Back After These Messages*

▶ **Clauses**

Practice

Read the sentences. Underline the adverb clause in each sentence.

5. Whenever Mike's dad has a new job, Mike's family has to move.

6. They can't live in one place for very long unless Mike's dad gets a new assignment at the same location.

7. Once, everyone had to leave right after Mike's birthday party was over!

8. Mike can pack easily because he does not own a lot of stuff.

9. Mike hopes he can stay here until he goes to middle school.

10. Mike's parents also want to live here because they think it will be good for Mike and his brother.

Proofread

Read the paragraph. Underline all the adjective clauses. Circle all the adverb clauses.

Mike showed us all sorts of souvenirs that he has from different countries. His dad is a person who fixes things, so Mr. Schneider goes wherever the company has broken machinery. The machines that Mike's father likes to fix are the helicopters. He likes them because he has to pay attention to how the wires and circuits are connected in the engine. One of the helicopter pilots whom Mike talked to a lot gave him a patch that the pilots sew on their uniforms.

GRAMMAR AND USAGE

UNIT 5 Communication • **Lesson 2** *We'll Be Right Back After These Messages*

Avoiding Wordiness

Wordiness generally means using too many words to express an idea or to describe something. Wordiness can clutter your writing and confuse your readers. Here are two forms of wordiness.

Rule	**Example**
▶ One form of wordiness is **redundancy**. Redundancy is the use of too many words that have the same meaning (synonyms) to express or describe a single idea or thing.	▶ He <u>descended</u> <u>down</u> the stairs. (*Descend* means "to go down.") He <u>repeated</u> the directions <u>again</u>. (*Repeat* means "to do something again.")
▶ Another form of wordiness is using many words when you need only a few.	▶ *Wordy:* I would like to talk to you <u>in regard to</u> your homework. *A better way to say it:* I would like to talk to you <u>about</u> your homework. *Wordy:* I was late <u>because of the fact that</u> the bus didn't stop for me. *A better way to say it:* I was late <u>because</u> the bus didn't stop for me.

**Read the following sentences. Underline
the words or phrases that are redundant.**

1. Almost everybody, except for a few people, understood the lesson.

2. I saw a sailboat far away, in the distance.

3. I thought in my head that we would win the game.

4. We watched the big huge cloud cover the sun.

5. George wanted to be home alone by himself, but his mother wouldn't allow it.

Avoiding Wordiness

Practice

Rewrite each sentence to reduce wordiness.

6. We descended the stairs down to the basement.

_____

7. The baking lesson went well except for the fact that I spilled a bag of flour.

_____

8. The poodle's little tiny paws made dirty, muddy tracks on the clean, sparkling floor.

_____

9. During the last two weeks, we have had fourteen out of fourteen days of rain.

_____

10. John began to think thoughts of winning the basketball trophy.

_____

11. When the sun goes down at sunset, we are going fishing.

_____

12. We parked our car in the garage and left it there while we went to the science museum.

_____

WRITER'S CRAFT

Direct Objects

Rule	Example
▶ The noun or pronoun in a sentence that *receives* the action of the verb is the **direct object.** To identify the direct object in a sentence, find the verb and ask *Whom?* or *What?* If *what* or *whom* can't be answered, the sentence has no direct object.	▶ Frank cooked **an omelet** this morning. (Frank cooked *what?* An omelet.) He cleaned after breakfast. (He cleaned *what* or *whom?* There is no answer, so there is no direct object in the sentence.)

Read the sentences. Circle each verb that has a direct object. Write the letter *D* over each direct object. Write "no direct object" on the line if the sentences don't have one.

1. Rosa memorized her lines for the play at school.

   _____

2. She also practiced the dance steps with Helen, Maureen,

   and me. _____

3. Her brother Antonio made funny faces at us.

   _____

4. We were nervous about our performance that night.

   _____

5. Rosa performed a beautiful dance.

   _____

GRAMMAR AND USAGE

Practice

Read the sentences. Circle each direct object.

6. Rosa's mom or dad takes her to dance class every week.

7. Rosa took Antonio to her class.

8. Rosa introduced him to her dance teacher.

9. Antonio watched the dancers.

10. Rosa has performed dances with many people.

11. She likes to learn new steps from more experienced dancers.

Proofread

Read the paragraph. Circle each verb that has a direct object. Write the letter *D* over each direct object.

After the play, Rosa's parents took us to a sandwich shop for a celebration. Rosa shared her allowance with Antonio so he could buy a sandwich. Antonio asked his father if he could add some cheese to his sandwich. His father said yes. He ordered cheese on his sandwich, too. Antonio adds swiss cheese to his sandwich. Rosa prefers tomatoes on hers.

Structure of a Business Letter

A business letter is formal in tone and is addressed to a person who represents a company or organization. The purpose of your letter will determine what will go in the body. Here are different types of business letters and the kind of information each should contain.

Write a **letter of request** to order something or ask for information.

▶ State what you need.

▶ State your appreciation.

Write a **letter of complaint** to let someone know there is a problem and you want it fixed.

▶ State the problem.

▶ State the action you expect them to take to fix the problem.

Write a **letter of opinion** to let someone know about an issue that concerns you.

▶ State your opinion.

▶ Give your reasons.

▶ State the action, if any, the reader should take.

All business letters should include the following parts: heading, inside address, salutation, body, closing, and your signature. Make sure you use capitalization and punctuation correctly in all parts of your business letter.

Read the following subjects of a business letter. Write <u>request</u>, <u>complaint</u>, or <u>concern</u> next to the type of letter you might write.

1._____ You want to tell the owner of a grocery store that you don't like a new cereal she is selling.

2._____ You want to ask the owner of a grocery store to sell a particular brand of cereal.

UNIT 5 Communication • **Lesson 3** *Breaking into Print*

Structure of a Business Letter

Practice

Write a business letter based on the information below. Make sure you include all the parts of a business letter. Use capitalization and punctuation correctly in your letter.

Your class is visiting Washington, D.C., April 1 to 4. Write a letter to your senator asking if he or she can arrange a tour of the Capitol.

_____

_____

_____

_____

_____

_____

_____

_____

_____

_____

_____

_____

_____

WRITER'S CRAFT

Fragments, Run-On, Rambling, and Awkward Sentences

Rule	**Example**
▶ A group of words that does not express a complete thought is not a sentence, but a **fragment.**	▶ Harry's new puppy. Didn't eat her food.
▶ A sentence with no punctuation or coordinating conjunctions between two or more independent clauses is a **run-on sentence.**	▶ The puppy has been quiet all day Harry doesn't know if she's sick or not.
▶ In a **rambling sentence,** a writer strings together many thoughts. Rambling sentences often have many *ands* in them.	▶ Harry kept his puppy warm and he called the vet and the vet told Harry to give the dog some medicine.
▶ An **awkward sentence** is a sentence that does not read well.	▶ Harry gave the medicine to the dog and she began to get better, so Harry was very happy about that.

Read the sentences. Write either *fragment* or *run-on sentence* in the blank.

1. From 1941 to 1945, Native Americans. _____

2. These soldiers were members of the Comanche people they helped the United States protect its military secrets

   during the war. _____

3. The Germans didn't know anything about the Comanche language hearing more words that were different confused

   them even more. _____

Fragments, Run-On, Rambling, and Awkward Sentences

Practice

Read the sentences. Write either *awkward sentence* or *rambling sentence* in the blank.

4. Many people who are blind read by using a system of raised dots known as Braille invented in 1826.

   _____

5. Louis Braille invented this system and he was French and

   he was a teenager. _____

6. They use their fingers to make letters and words and each letter and word has a different sign and it takes a long

   time to learn to sign well. _____

7. American Sign Language is one type of sign language that

   is a system of sign language. _____

Proofread

Read the paragraph. Correct any fragments, run-on sentences, rambling sentences, or awkward sentences. Use proofreading marks to make the corrections.

   Signs and symbols. Tell people many things. Signs can tell us when to stop and they can show us how to get out of a building, and they can also help us get to places like the store, the library, or a relative's house. Signs also keep people from getting into trouble it isn't a good idea to drink out of a bottle that has the symbol for poison on it. If someone drinks poison, that person needs to go to the hospital so doctors can take the poison out of the person's body so he or she doesn't get sick from the poison.

GRAMMAR AND USAGE

Outlining

An **outline** is the plan writers use to organize their ideas and notes before they start writing.

Organize your information into main topics and subtopics. There should be at least two main topics and at least two subtopics, or none at all, under each main topic.

Step 1. Write a title for your project. What is your project about?_____ **Antarctica**

Step 2. Decide on the main topics. Check the headings on your note cards. The main headings are numbered with Roman numerals (I, II, III, IV, etc.).

Step 3. Decide how each main topic can be divided. These are subtopics under your main topics. They are indented and labeled with capital letters (A, B, C).

Step 4. You can break your subtopics into smaller subtopics. Each of these smaller subtopics is indented again and labeled with Arabic numerals (1, 2, 3, and so on).

I. Lands
   A. East Antarctica
     1. Size
     2. Land forms
   B. West Antarctica
II. Natural Resources
   A. Minerals
     1. Coal
     2. Ore deposits
   B. Plants
     1. Lichens
     2. Moss
     3. Flowering Plants

Create a form for an outline, showing where the title goes and how main topics and subtopics are labeled and arranged.

_____

_____

_____

_____

_____

_____

_____

Practice

Create an outline for a report on life in the New England colonies based on the information below.

Ways colonists earned a living   In town
Farming   Taking part in government
Trapping   Doing household chores
In the country   Blacksmithing
Ways colonists spent other time   Shopkeeping

_____

_____

_____

_____

_____

_____

_____

_____

_____

WRITER'S CRAFT

Drawing Conclusions

Focus Drawing conclusions helps readers get more information from a story.

> ▶ **Drawing conclusions** means taking small pieces of information, or details, about a character or story event and using them to make a statement about that character or event.
>
> ▶ The conclusion may not be stated in the text but should be supported from the text.

Identify

Look through "Louis Braille: The Boy Who Invented Books for the Blind" for details you can use to draw conclusions. Choose and write two different groups of details from the story and the page number. Then write the conclusion for each.

1. Page: _____   Detail: _____

_____

Detail: _____

_____

Conclusion: _____

_____

2. Page: _____   Detail: _____

_____

Detail: _____

_____

Conclusion: _____

► **Drawing Conclusions**

Practice

Read the paragraph below. Draw a conclusion based on the text. Then write two sentences with details that support the conclusion.

What Hassan noticed first was the noise. Stepping through the double doors, he fought against the wall of sound made by hundreds of wheels spinning on the hardwood floor. And it was dark in here—darker than he had expected. Nervously, Hassan followed Dominic to the skate rental counter.

Conclusion: _____

_____

Detail: _____

_____

Detail: _____

_____

Apply

Write two sentences with details about a trip you have taken or would like to take. Then draw a conclusion about the trip from the details in the sentences. Write the conclusion in the space below.

Sentence: _____

_____

Sentence: _____

_____

Conclusion: _____

_____

COMPREHENSION

Agreement in Sentences

Rule	Example
▶ For a sentence to have **subject-verb agreement,** the verb must agree with the subject in the sentence.	▶ Dana **likes** to read a book before she goes to bed. Eric and Mark **finish** their homework every evening.
▶ Pronouns and their antecedents must also agree in number. An **antecedent** is the noun that a pronoun refers to in a sentence. If a pronoun refers to a singular noun in a sentence, the pronoun must be singular. If a pronoun refers to a plural noun, the pronoun must be plural. When pronouns and their antecedents match up this way, a sentence has **pronoun-antecedent agreement.**	▶ The **cat** ate so much tuna that **it** got sick. There were a lot of **rules** about phrases, and I realized I had no idea what **they** meant.
▶ **Modifiers** are words that describe or add to the meaning of nouns, pronouns, and verbs. Modifiers should be placed near the noun, pronoun, or verb that they are describing.	▶ Eric yelled **loudly** that he had solved the problem. (**Loudly** is a modifier; it tells how Eric yelled in the sentence.)

Read the sentences. Circle the correct verb or pronoun in each set of parentheses.

1. The students (speaks, speak) only Spanish during class.

2. Señora Martinez (believes, believe) this will help them (learns, learn) to pronounce words correctly.

3. The girls (offers, offer) to help their classmates if (they, them) (have, has) trouble with an assignment.

UNIT 5 Communication • **Lesson 5** *Louis Braille: The Boy Who Invented Books for the Blind*

Agreement in Sentences

Practice

Read the sentences. Underline the words that modify the noun, pronoun, or verb circled in each sentence.

4. Did the architect tell you that the plans for the house would be (finished) quickly?

5. A group of business (people) from the company told me that the plans are almost finished.

6. The paint will be stripped off the walls, and we'll choose a new (color) for the dining room.

7. Mitch told us that the door could be (fixed) easily.

8. One construction worker (yelled) angrily when he hit his thumb with a hammer.

9. The cold (metal) hurt even more because the worker was outside.

Proofread

Read the paragraph. Circle the correct verb or pronoun in each set of parentheses. Write an X over each underlined modifier that does NOT modify a word correctly.

Mark, Eric, and Dawn (goes, go) to the arena every week to see their favorite hockey team (play, plays) a game. The kids like to watch the game as (they, them) hungrily (eat, eats) pretzels hungrily. Mark always (screams, scream) until (he, they) (have, has) no voice left, but he (has, have) fun anyway. Eric didn't want to tear his ticket stub colorful because it looked very colorful. Dawn (think, thinks) (her, she) crazy brothers (is, are) crazy!

Writing a Bibliography

A **bibliography** is a list of resources about a subject. It includes books, magazines, or other written materials used for research. Writers provide this information for two reasons: 1) the reader will know where the information came from and; 2) the reader will know where to look for more information.

As you do research for a project, make a note card for each book or article you use. Write the information in this form:

▶ The author's full name (last name, first name, middle initial or name) followed by a period

▶ The title of the book underlined and followed by a period

▶ The name of the publisher, followed by a comma

▶ The date of publication, followed by a period.

Krakauer, Jon. Into Thin Air: A Personal Account of the Mt. Everest Disaster. Villard, 1997.

When you put your bibliography together at the end of your paper, put entries in alphabetical order by the last name of the author.

If there is no author's name, list the work alphabetically by title. (If the first word is *The*, *A*, or *An*, use the second word of the title.) If there is only an editor listed, list alphabetically by editor's last name.

Try It! Write these authors' names in alphabetical order.

A.A. Milne   _____
Lewis Carroll
Ogden Nash   _____
A.E. Houseman
                        _____

                        _____

▶ **Writing a Bibliography**

Practice

Write these items in alphabetical order and in bibliographical form.

The Universal Almanac 2001 published by Andrews and McNeel in 2000

The Americans: The Colonial Experience by Daniel Boorstin, published by Vintage/Random House, 1974

A People's History of the United States by Howard Zinn, HarperPerennial, 1990

_____

_____

_____

_____

_____

_____

_____

_____

_____

_____

WRITER'S CRAFT

Review

▶ Phrases

Read the sentences. Write *participial phrase*, *prepositional phrase*, or *appositive phrase* to describe the phrase underlined in each sentence.

1. The crust of the Earth is divided into large pieces called

   plates. _____

2. Moving in many different directions, the plates sometimes

   hit each other. _____

3. A seismograph, a type of scientific instrument, measures

   how strong an earthquake is. _____

4. Observing each time the Earth shakes, scientists gain

   valuable information. _____

▶ Clauses

Read the sentences. Write *adjective clause* or *adverb clause* to describe the clause underlined in each sentence.

5. Jared took out the trash as soon as he got home from

   karate class. _____

6. Jared learned how to perform some movements in class

   that were very difficult, but his instructor told him to keep

   practicing them. _____

7. A lot of people in Jared's class were teenagers and adults

   who had taken karate for many years. _____

Direct Objects

Read the sentences. Circle all verbs that have a direct object. Write *D* over each direct object.

8. Amanda's father gave her a surprise on her birthday.

9. He baked chocolate cupcakes all by himself.

10. Her mom baked the cupcakes for her birthday.

Sentence Fragments, Run-on Sentences, Rambling Sentences, and Awkward Sentences

Read the sentences. Write *sentence fragments, run-on sentence, rambling sentence,* or *awkward sentence* in the blank.

11. The first roller coaster that came to the United States was

named "Gravity Road" it was 18 miles long. _____

12. It dropped people. More than 1,200 feet. _____

13. The roller coaster was in Pennsylvania and it was
supposed to carry coal, but people thought it looked like

fun and they started asking for rides. _____

Agreement in Sentences

Read the paragraph. Circle the correct verb or pronoun in the parentheses. Write an X over each underlined modifier that does NOT modify a word correctly.

Computers (has, have) been used to (solve, solves) complicated math problems complicated. However, (them, they) can do more than just math! People (communicates, communicate) with each other by using computers.

GRAMMAR AND USAGE

Developing Persuasive Writing

Persuasive writing is used to convince readers to think, feel, or act a certain way. There are different ways to persuade readers. One way to persuade is to support your opinion mainly with *facts* and *reasons*. Another way to appeal to readers is through their *interests* or *feelings*.

Organization

Once you decide how you will persuade readers, you must choose a way to organize your information and ideas to make your argument most convincing. One way to do this is by **order of importance**.

In persuasive writing, often it helps to present your facts and reasons from least important to most important.

Example

▶ The school cafeteria should serve pizza for lunch. Pizza is a healthful food. It has ingredients from most food groups: the crust is from the bread group; the tomato sauce and mushrooms are from the fruit and vegetable group; the cheese is from the dairy group. Pizza has the vitamins and protein we need. It tastes good, and children like it. It should be on the menu.

For each topic below, write the most effective approach—facts or feelings—to writing a persuasive piece and explain why.

1. You are writing to convince your grandparents to visit you on your birthday.

   _____

2. You want to convince the school board that they should put more money into art and music instruction.

   _____

UNIT 5 Communication • **Lesson 6** *My Two Drawings*

▶ **Developing Persuasive Writing**

Practice

Write a persuasive paragraph on the topic below. Choose your approach—facts or feelings—and organize your reasons in order of importance.

You've just met the new student at your school. Convince him or her that your school is a great place.

_____

_____

_____

_____

_____

_____

_____

_____

_____

_____

_____

_____

_____

WRITER'S CRAFT

UNIT 6 A Changing America • **Lesson I** *Early America*

Classifying and Categorizing

Focus Good readers classify items into categories as they read to help them organize information and understand what they read.

> **Classifying** means arranging people, places, or things into different groups or **categories.** When classifying and categorizing people, ideas, places, or things,
> ▶ name the categories, or groups, for similar items.
> ▶ list any items that fit the category.
> **Early American Colonies** ◄—— *Category*
> Massachusetts
> Rhode Island
> Maryland
> Some items can be put in more than one category.
>
> | **Early American Colonies** | **States of the United States** |
> |---|---|
> | Massachusetts | Massachusetts |
> | Rhode Island | Rhode Island |
> | Maryland | Maryland |

Identify

Look through "Early America" and list all the items that fit the categories below.

1. Explorers to America before Columbus in 1492

_____

_____

2. Nationality of explorers to America in the 1490s and early 1500s

_____

_____

▶ **Classifying and Categorizing**

3. Countries that colonists came from in 1700

_____

_____

4. Names of colonies

_____

_____

Practice

Name a category that best fits each of the groups of items below. Write the category in the spaces provided.

5. Bananas, grapes, apples, strawberries _____

6. Baseball, basketball, golf, tennis _____

7. Lion tamers, clowns, flying trapeze artists, elephant trainers

_____

8. Richard Nixon, Ulysses S. Grant, Abraham Lincoln, Calvin Coolidge

_____

Apply

Think about the subjects you learn in school, such as social studies and math. Choose your favorite subject and list any items that you might use for that subject, such as a compass for math and maps for geography. Write the subject and the items in the spaces below.

My favorite subject is: _____

Items: _____

COMPREHENSION

Identifying and Using Parts of Speech

▶ Nouns and Verbs

Read the paragraph. Circle all of the nouns. Underline all of the verbs.

In the early nineteenth century, many Americans wanted to move away from the coast and find new land to farm and live on. However, the Appalachian Mountains were in their path. One man, who would later become governor of New York, thought it might be a good idea to build a canal.

▶ Possessive Nouns, Pronouns, Adjectives, and Adverbs

Read the paragraph. Circle all of the pronouns, possessive nouns, and possessive pronouns. Underline all of the adjectives. Draw a box or a square around all of the adverbs. Put apostrophes where they are needed.

His name was DeWitt Clinton. Some people thought his idea was foolish. They called the canal "Clintons Ditch" and said that it would fail miserably. The state government of New York gave Mr. Clinton permission to build his canal anyway.

▶ Plural Nouns

Read the paragraph. Circle the correct plural form of each noun in parentheses.

The new canal would run between the (citys, cities) of Albany and Buffalo, New York. When it was finished, (teams, teames) of (mulees, mules) would use (ropes, ropees) to pull (boates, boats) along the canal. Many people started new (businesses, business) near the canal as it was being built. Sometimes (thiefs, thieves) would rob these (companies, companys).

UNIT 6 A Changing America • **Lesson I** *Early America*

Identifying and Using Parts of Speech

All Parts of Speech

Read the paragraph. Write all of the nouns, pronouns, verbs, adjectives, and adverbs in the chart below.

The canal's width was forty feet, its depth was four feet, and it had sides that were built on a slope. Workers had to stand in a swamp to build one part of the canal. The leeches and mosquitoes that lived in the swamp bit many of the workers and made them very sick. Doctors tried many treatments until they discovered that bark from a tree in Peru was helping the workers feel better. This tree's bark contained a substance called quinine, which is still used to make medicine. Even though the canal had many problems, Mr. Clinton opened one section of it in October 1819. Today, we call this waterway the Erie Canal.

Nouns
Verbs
Plural and Possesive Nouns
Pronouns
Adjectives
Adverbs

GRAMMAR AND USAGE

UNIT 6 A Changing America • **Lesson I** *Early America*

End Rhyme

In many poems, the last words in certain lines rhyme. This is called **end rhyme.** You probably have heard end rhyme in some poems, songs and nursery rhymes. Here are two lines of a familiar nursery rhyme that has end rhyme.

> Little Miss Muffet
> Sat on a tuffet

There are different end rhyme patterns. In some poems, the last words in the first and second lines rhyme and the last words in the third and fourth lines rhyme. In some poems, only the last words in the second and fourth lines rhyme.

 **Read the rhyme below. Write the words in each line that are end rhymes in the space provided.**

Vintery, mintery, cutery, corn,
Apple seed and apple thorn;
Wire, briar, limber lock,
Three geese in a flock.
One flew east,
And one flew west,
And one flew over the cuckoo's nest.

_____

_____

_____

▶ **End Rhyme**

Practice

For each line, write a second line that rhymes.

1. When I sit at the window and stare

_____

2. If in the world I could do

_____

3. In a park, by the lake

_____

4. A bright and lazy summer's day

_____

5. One day at the county fair

_____

6. In the town where I was born

_____

Here are the first two lines of a poem. Write two more lines so that the first and third, and second and fourth lines rhyme.

I watch my cats sleep lazily on the chair;
They twitch and smile while they dream.

_____

_____

_____

_____

WRITER'S CRAFT

Internal Rhyme

> ▶ **Rule**
> **Internal rhyme** rhymes the last word in a line with another word in the middle of the *same* line.

> ▶ **Example**
> Apples golden and delicious
> Hung on <u>trees</u>, caught the <u>breeze</u>.

Underline the internal rhyme in each example.

1. "You can't be bored," the teacher roared.

2. Does any insect have self-respect?

3. The babysitter pitched a no-hitter.

4. "I think," said the balladeer, "I must find a new career."

5. In a gold and white costume the dancer walked into the room.

6. The brown dog ran behind the van.

7. Sam and Max are there, and they make quite a pair.

8. That lazy cat is crazy!

9. The waiter brought the water later.

10. I looked at the book he took.

11. Josh knows Sally who lives in the valley.

12. At eight, Craig loaded the crate.

▶ **Internal Rhyme**

Practice

Write at least two words that rhyme with each word below.

13. angle _____

14. snake _____

15. crunch _____

16. wire _____

17. plate _____

18. four _____

Use the sets of rhyming words you created above to write sentences with internal rhyme.

19. _____

20. _____

21. _____

22. _____

23. _____

24. _____

WRITER'S CRAFT

Making Inferences

Focus   Readers make inferences about characters and events to understand the total picture in a story.

An **inference** is a statement about a character or event in a story. To make an inference, the reader uses

▶ **information** from the story, such as examples, facts, reasons, and descriptions.

▶ **personal experience or knowledge,** which are the individual memories and experiences you bring to the story.

Identify

Look through "The Voyage of the Mayflower." Choose a character or a story event and make an inference about it. Write the character's name or story event in the spaces below. Then write the information from the story, the page number, and personal experience or knowledge and make an inference.

Character or story event: _____

_____

Page: _____   Information from the text: _____

_____

_____

_____

Personal experience or knowledge: _____

_____

Inference: _____

_____

Making Inferences

Practice

Read the paragraph and make an inference. In the spaces below, write the inference and the information and personal experience or knowledge you used to make the inference.

Marisa takes notes on the information her teachers give in class. She carefully writes down the homework assignments in her calendar book. When she gets home from school, she has a snack of fruit and milk. She then goes over her notes and does her homework. Marisa organizes her friends for a study group before tests. When she gets her report card, she runs home, eager to show it to her family.

Inference: _____

Information from the paragraph: _____

_____

Personal experience or knowledge: _____

_____

Apply

Write a short paragraph about the passengers of the *Mayflower*. Use sentences with information that a reader could use to make an inference about them. Use a separate sheet of paper if you need more space.

_____

_____

_____

_____

_____

_____

COMPREHENSION

Capitalization and Punctuation in Words and Sentences

▶ Capitalization, Periods, and Commas

Read the paragraph. Place capital letters, periods, and commas where they are needed. Use proofreading marks to make the corrections.

in 1866 twelve thousand men came to omaha nebraska to help build a transcontinental railroad in the united states These men worked on steamboats unloaded supplies on the docks and laid rails to make the railroad Some of the workers had come from ireland or they were new immigrants from other countries many others had fought in the civil war The men often wore scarves large hats high boots and checked shirts when they worked on the railroad.

▶ Capitalization, Colons, Commas, Parentheses, and Periods

Read the paragraph. Place capital letters, colons, commas, parentheses, and periods where they are needed. Use proofreading marks to make the corrections.

The us government wanted the railroad to connect the atlantic ocean with the pacific ocean. While workers in omaha were laying rails toward the west more workers were also building the railroad toward the east. The sections of rails would fit together at promontory point utah. The workers even had nicknames for themselves "tarriers" for the group heading to the west the men from omaha and "crocker's pets" for the group heading to the east.

UNIT 6 A Changing America • **Lesson 2** *The Voyage of the Mayflower*

Capitalization and Punctuation in Words and Sentences

MECHANICS

Capitalization, Commas, End Punctuation, Quotation Marks, and Underlining

Read the sentences. Use end punctuation, quotation marks, and underlining where they are needed in each sentence. Place commas and capital letters where they are missing. Use proofreading marks to make the corrections.

1. What kinds of food do you think the railroad workers ate for breakfast

2. Wow I read that cooks sometimes got into lots of trouble if the workers didn't like the food

3. If they were very angry the workers would often run the cook completely out of the camp

4. The book From Sea to Shining Sea by amy l. cohn says that meat potatoes fruit vegetables pie and coffee were usually served for breakfast Do you think the workers sang the song I've Been Working on the Railroad as they were laying the rails

Apostrophes, Commas, Hyphens, and Semicolons

Read the paragraph. Place apostrophes, commas, hyphens, and semicolons where they are needed. Use proofreading marks to make the corrections.

Railroad workers didnt just throw rails onto the ground to make the railroad. First they had to use blasting powder wheelbarrows and hand shovels to move dirt and rock out of their way. After that pieces of wood called "ties" were placed on the ground workers laid the rails on top of the ties. The rails were about twenty eight feet long and they were held down with iron spikes. Since these rails were made of iron they were very heavy but the workers worked together so they could lay the track quickly.

UNIT 6 A Changing America • **Lesson 2** *The Voyage of the Mayflower*

Figurative Language

Figurative language is a use of words that relate a thing to another thing or idea. Using figurative language in your writing helps the reader form vivid mental pictures of abstract things or ideas.

Figurative is the opposite of *literal*. That is, figurative language does not have a factual meaning.

Another term for figurative language is **figures of speech.** There are many figures of speech that can make your writing more interesting.

Rule	**Example**
▶ A **simile** uses the word *like* or *as* to compare two things that are not alike.	▶ The man's head was smooth <u>as a bowling ball</u>.
▶ A **metaphor** compares two things that are not alike without using *like* or *as*.	▶ The waves <u>galloped</u> to shore.
▶ **Personification** gives human qualities to an animal, object, or idea.	▶ The wind <u>whispered</u> its secrets, but the trees responded with <u>laughter</u>.

 **Try It!** List the figure of speech—simile, metaphor, or personification—used in each sentence below.

1. When Lucy laughed, she honked like a goose. _____

2. The engine purred when John's mother finished fixing it. _____

3. "Why doesn't anyone understand me?" the little mouse

   cried. _____

4. The computer stubbornly refused to do what I wanted. _____

5. His hair was tangled and limp like cooked spaghetti. _____

▶ Figurative Language

Practice

Write sentences using simile, metaphor, or personification based on the instructions for each sentence.

6. Write a sentence about a flower. Use personification.

_____

_____

7. Write a sentence about a piece of furniture. Use personification.

_____

_____

8. Write a sentence that compares two slippery things. Use a simile.

_____

_____

9. Write a sentence that compares a person to an animal. Use a simile.

_____

_____

10. Write a sentence using a weather metaphor.

_____

11. Write a sentence using color as a metaphor.

_____

12. Write a sentence using a plant as a metaphor.

_____

WRITER'S CRAFT

Words, Phrases, Clauses, and Modifiers

Dependent Clauses and Prepositional Phrases

Read the paragraph. Underline each dependent clause. Circle each prepositional phrase, and draw an X through the object of the preposition.

Between 1890 and 1920, more than twenty million people immigrated to the United States. These immigrants were people who had decided to leave their own countries and come live in America. Some of them came here because there was danger where they lived. Others were hoping to find work so that they could send money back to their families. To stay in this country, however, many immigrants had to visit Ellis Island first.

Appositive Phrases, Participial Phrases, and Direct Objects

Read the paragraph. Underline each appositive phrase. Circle each participial phrase. Write a *D* over each direct object.

Ellis Island, an island in New York City's harbor, was the largest immigration center in the world. Ships loaded with passengers arrived each day. Waiting nervously, hundreds of people stood in line. Doctors examined the passengers and asked questions about each person's health. If anyone had a contagious disease, an illness that can spread easily and make others sick, he or she wasn't allowed to stay in the United States.

One-Word Modifiers, Direct Objects

Read the paragraph. Circle each modifier. Underline the word that each one modifies. Write a D over each direct object.

Ellis Island was a very loud, busy place. The immigrants spoke different languages. Doctors and workers could not easily understand what people were saying to them. Hands and fists waved quickly through the air as the immigrants answered many questions. Were they healthy or sick? Did they have a new job in the United States? Were they rich or poor? The workers took the immigrants' old money and gave American money to them. Once they answered questions and received American money, the immigrants could leave crowded Ellis Island and live in a big city, a small town, or any other place they wanted.

Adjectives and Adverb Clauses

Read the paragraph. Underline each adjective clause. Circle each adverb clause.

When the Great Depression began, life became difficult for many Americans. Banks had to close because they couldn't give people or businesses their money. Since businesses didn't have any money, they couldn't pay the people who worked for them. There were long lines for bread and soup that were given away for free. While these events happened over fifty years ago, many Americans still remember what it was like to live during that time.

Alliteration means repeating the consonant sounds at the beginning of words. You have heard it in tongue-twisters:

Peter Piper picked a peck of pickled peppers.

You will also find it in many poems and in advertising.

Try It!

Match the word in column A with its alliteration partner in column B.

A	B
_____ **1.** baby's	**a.** python
_____ **2.** candid	**b.** house
_____ **3.** pet	**c.** tale
_____ **4.** haunted	**d.** breath
_____ **5.** tall	**e.** camera
_____ **6.** master	**f.** days
_____ **7.** dog	**g.** mind
_____ **8.** red	**h.** glue
_____ **9.** gooey	**i.** salamander
_____ **10.** sad	**j.** rooster

UNIT 6 A Changing America • **Lesson 3** *Pocohontas*

Practice

For each animal, write an alliterative adjective.

11. wombat _____

12. turtle _____

13. rooster _____

14. deer _____

15. horse _____

16. bat _____

17. colt _____

18. gorilla _____

19. kangaroo _____

20. llama _____

Choose three of the animals above. Write a sentence about each animal using the alliterative adjectives listed above.

_____

_____

_____

_____

_____

_____

_____

_____

WRITER'S CRAFT

UNIT 6 A Changing America • **Lesson 3** *Pocohontas*

Assonance

Rule	Example
▶ **Assonance** is another term relating to sounds in words. It is the repetition of *vowel sounds* in words. Sometimes it is called *vowel rhyme*. Assonance affects the sound of your writing when read aloud. It is often used in poetry.	▶ The <u>boat</u> is <u>so</u> far away. (Long *o* sound is repeated.)
▶ With assonance, the words may rhyme (red, head) or may just have the same vowel sound (red, test).	▶ The freshly <u>baked</u> <u>cake</u> <u>tastes</u> <u>great</u>. (Long *a* sound is repeated).

 **Try It!** Match the color word in column A with its assonance partner in column B.

	A		B
____	**1.** Blue	**a.**	Cloud
____	**2.** Pink	**b.**	Mood
____	**3.** Yellow	**c.**	Haze
____	**4.** Brown	**d.**	Ring
____	**5.** Black	**e.**	Bench
____	**6.** Purple	**f.**	Shack
____	**7.** Green	**g.**	Turtle
____	**8.** Gray	**h.**	Wheat

UNIT 6 A Changing America • **Lesson 3** *Pocohontas*

Practice

Write a group of four or five words for each of the
words listed below that show assonance.

9. paid _____

10. seen _____

11. flight _____

12. boat _____

13. judge _____

14. proud _____

15. sat _____

Choose three groups of words from the list above and
write a sentence from each that shows assonance.

_____

_____

_____

_____

_____

_____

_____

_____

_____

_____

WRITER'S CRAFT

Compare and Contrast

Focus Writers sometimes compare and contrast things, events, or characters to make a story clearer and more interesting.

> ▶ To **compare** means to tell how things, events, or characters are alike.
> ▶ To **contrast** means to tell how things, events, or characters are different.

Identify

Look through "Martha Helps the Rebel." Describe how Martha and her mother are alike and describe how they are different in the spaces below.

1. How Martha and her mother are alike:

_____

_____

_____

_____

2. How Martha and her mother are different:

_____

_____

_____

_____

UNIT 6 A Changing America • **Lesson 4** *Martha Helps the Rebel*

Compare and Contrast

Practice

Look at the word pairs below. Write how the items in each pair are different and how they are alike.

3. digital watch   analog watch

Different: _____

_____

Alike: _____

_____

4. car   horse

Different: _____

_____

Alike: _____

_____

Apply

Write a paragraph comparing and contrasting two things, events, or characters. Describe how they are the same and how they are different.

_____

_____

_____

_____

_____

_____

COMPREHENSION

Understanding and Combining Sentences

▶ Kinds of Sentences

Read the sentences. Write *declarative, exclamatory, interrogative,* or *imperative* in the blank next to the sentence.

1. Did you know that one of the very first baseball games was played in Hoboken, New Jersey, in June 1846?

   _____

2. Please tell me all about the game. _____

3. The New York Nine beat the New York Knickerbockers by

   the score of 23–1. _____

4. Gosh, that game wasn't very close! _____

▶ Types of Sentences

Read the sentences. Write *simple, compound,* or *complex* in the blank next to the sentence.

5. The first professional baseball team was the Cincinnati

   Red Stockings. _____

6. Because the Red Stockings didn't lose a game when they toured the United States in 1869, the team was very

   popular. _____

7. The National League was organized, and more people

   began to come to baseball games. _____

► **Combining Sentences**

Read each set of sentences or clauses and combine each set into a compound or complex sentence. Add coordinating and subordinating conjunctions and change any capital letters or punctuation that needs to be changed. Use proofreading marks to make the corrections.

8. Players started to wear baseball gloves in the 1880s. They were not as large as today's gloves.

9. Batters could ask the pitcher to throw the ball "high" or "low. Pitchers could only throw the ball underhand.

10. Because ushers had to go into the stands to find baseballs finishing a game was sometimes impossible.

► **Sentence Fragments, Run-On Sentences, Rambling Sentences, and Awkward Sentences**

Read the following *fragments, run-on sentences, rambling sentences,* or *awkward sentences*. Correct the problems in each by using proofreading marks.

11. Jackie Robinson. Was the first African-American to play major league baseball.

12. He joined the Brooklyn Dodgers and Jackie had played in a baseball league for African-American players and Mr. Robinson had also played sports while he was in college.

13. He worked very hard to not react to what fans said, but that wasn't always easy and sometimes even the other players didn't like him.

Rhythm

Rhythm is the pattern of accented and unaccented syllables often heard in lines of poetry or in sentences of some prose writing.

▶ Rhythm often helps set the mood and tone in a piece of writing. Also, rhythm can express movement and sound, making a piece of writing come alive for a reader through both sight and sound. Read aloud the following lines from a familiar children's rhyme. The accented syllables are marked. Can you hear the rhythm?

> Híckory, díckory, dóck,
> The móuse ran up the clóck.

▶ Writers create the rhythm by their choice of words. The sound of the letters contributes to the rhythm. Harder sounds such as 't' or 'k' create a harder, faster beat. Soft sounds such as 's' or 'sh' slow the pace.

 **For each line below, write another line that has the same rhythm.**

1. Watch the children come and go

_____

2. Sleeping soundly through the night

_____

3. Humpty Dumpty sat on a wall

_____

Practice

Write a poem or two paragraphs about the movement or
sounds of nature, a ship, an animal, a machine, or some
other thing that you can picture or hear vividly. Make
the rhythm in your lines or sentences bring your images
to life.

_____

_____

_____

_____

_____

_____

_____

_____

_____

_____

_____

_____

_____

_____

_____

_____

WRITER'S CRAFT

Onomatopoeia

Rule	**Examples**
▶ **Onomatopoeia** is a figure of speech. It is the use of a word that imitates a sound.	▶ The bacon <u>sizzled</u> in the pan. The bees <u>buzzed</u> angrily.
▶ Onomatopoeia can make your writing come alive, especially when you read it aloud. These sound words help the reader hear the things you describe in your story or poem.	

 **Try It!** Write a sound word (onomatopoeia) for each of these objects or actions.

1. Bell _____

2. Snake _____

3. Broom _____

4. Tree falling _____

5. Pebble dropping into water _____

Write a word or action that each of these sound words reminds you of.

6. Screech _____

7. Squeak _____

8. Whirr _____

9. Crack _____

10. Honk _____

Comprehension and Language Arts Skills

▶ **Onomatopoeia**

Practice

Write a short paragraph or poem about nature, machines, an occupation, or another subject. Use as many examples of onomatopoeia as you can.

_____

_____

_____

_____

_____

_____

_____

_____

_____

_____

_____

_____

_____

_____

_____

_____

WRITER'S CRAFT

▶ Sequence

Focus Writers use signal words to help readers understand sequence. Sequence is the order of events in a story.

> Writers often use signal words called **time and order words** to show
>
> ▶ the passage of time in a story. Words such as *Tuesday*, *tomorrow*, and *the next day* show time.
>
> ▶ the order in which events take place. Words such as *first*, *then*, *so*, *when*, and *finally* show order.

Identify

Look through "Going West." Find two sentences with time words and two sentences with order words. Write the sentences and their page numbers in the spaces below. Underline the time and order words in each sentence.

1. Page: _____ Sentence with time words: _____

_____

2. Page: _____ Sentence with time words: _____

_____

3. Page: _____ Sentence with order words: _____

_____

4. Page: _____ Sentence with order words: _____

_____

 **Sequence**

Practice

Underline the words that signal time or order in each sentence.

5. We ate lunch at noon.

6. When the snow began, we all put on our hats and gloves and ran outside.

7. First, he inserted the key into the lock.

8. The next day, we all went to the movies.

9. Tomorrow we will do all of our homework and be very happy.

Apply

Write a paragraph about some of the things you did yesterday. Use time and order words to indicate when and in what order you did each thing.

_____

_____

_____

_____

_____

_____

_____

_____

_____

COMPREHENSION

Common Irregular Verbs

Came/Come, Rang/Rung, Sang/Sung

Read the paragraph. Correct any underlined verbs that are incorrect. Use proofreading marks to correct mistakes.

Melissa's family was moving, and everyone had <u>came</u> to her going-away party. The music was so loud that no one had heard the delivery person when he <u>rang</u> the doorbell with the pizza for the guests. Marcy, Melissa's best friend, <u>come</u> to the party after track practice. Melissa told her that they had <u>sang</u> four songs already and even her little brother Tony had <u>sung</u> "I'm a Little Teapot." Everyone <u>come</u> into the living room to listen to him, because they thought he sounded cute. Melissa's father told her that the telephone had <u>rang</u> while she had been talking to Marcy.

Took/Taken, Gave/Given, Ate/Eaten

Read the paragraph. Circle the correct verb in parentheses.

When she finished her phone call, Melissa checked to see if everyone had (ate, eaten) the rest of the pizza. Someone told her that her younger sister had (took, taken) the last piece while Melissa had been on the phone. Her parents reminded her that they had (gave, given) Melissa money so that she could order more pizza. Everyone cheered, and Melissa called the pizza place and (given, gave) someone her address again. After that, people (took, taken) a seat in the living room and watched movies until the pizza was delivered. Many of them (ate, eaten) carrots while they waited.

UNIT 6 A Changing America • **Lesson 5** *Going West*

Came/Come, Rang/Rung, Sang/Sung, Took/Taken, Gave/Given, Ate/Eaten, Went/Gone

Read the paragraph. Correct any underlined verbs that are incorrect. Use proofreading marks to make the corrections.

The doorbell had <u>rang</u>. The pizza was finally here. Melissa's friends felt like they hadn't <u>ate</u> in hours even though they had been <u>given</u> plenty of food. Melissa told her parents that she had <u>went</u> to check on Tony, and it sounded like he had <u>sang</u> himself to sleep. Her mother had <u>came</u> into the room to get a piece of pizza. She was surprised by what Melissa said, because Tony never <u>taken</u> a nap unless he was very tired. When she <u>went</u> down the hall to Tony's room to check on him, her husband <u>came</u> with her.

Went/Gone, Took/Taken, Gave/Given, Sang/Sung

Read the paragraph. Circle the correct verb in parentheses.

"Where did Tony go?" Melissa's father asked.

"I'm not sure where he (gone, went)," her mother answered, "but Melissa said he was tired after he (sung, sang) that song for her friends. Maybe he (taken, took) his blanket with him and has (gone, went) to his room to rest."

"He hasn't let that blanket out of his sight ever since Melissa (given, gave) it to him for his birthday last year."

"I know. Melissa had (taken, took) it away from him once so she could wash it, but Tony got so upset that she (gave, given) it right back."

GRAMMAR AND USAGE

UNIT 6   A Changing America • **Lesson 5** *Going West*

Repetition

▶ Repetition is the repeated use of words, sounds, a line of poetry, or a sentence in a story. Repetition helps create rhythm in a poem or in prose. It also adds emphasis to the idea being expressed.

Below, read the first two stanzas of the poem "Prophecy in Flame," by Frances Minturn Howard. Underline any repetition in this poem.

Grandfather wrote from Valley Forge,
"My dear, I miss you; times are harder;
The cheeses sent from home received,
A fine addition to our larder."

Grandfather wrote, "The volunteers
Are leaving—going home for haying;
We lose militia day by day;
But still a few of us are staying."

Why do you think the poet used repetition?

_____

_____

_____

_____

_____

_____

_____

Practice

Write a poem or paragraph about an event in American
history. Use repetition in your poem or paragraph.

_____

_____

_____

_____

_____

_____

_____

_____

_____

_____

_____

_____

_____

_____

_____

_____

WRITER'S CRAFT

UNIT 6 A Changing America • **Lesson 6** *The California Gold Rush*

Using Past, Present, and Future Tenses in Sentences

▶ Past to Present Tense

Read the paragraph. Change the underlined verbs from the past tense to the present tense. Write the verb above the past tense verb. Use proofreading marks to make the corrections.

Rebecca's stomach always <u>grumbled</u> when she <u>was</u> hungry. Her brother Mark <u>laughed</u> every time he <u>heard</u> it. Their sister Ruth <u>was</u> cooking dinner tonight. She <u>was</u> making a rice dish from Puerto Rico that <u>had</u> turmeric in it. Turmeric <u>made</u> the rice turn bright yellow. Rebecca <u>wondered</u> how the rice <u>was</u> going to taste.

▶ Present to Past Tense

Read the paragraph. Change the underlined verbs from the present tense to the past tense. Write the verb above the present tense verb. Use proofreading marks to make the corrections.

"This dinner is not good!" Mark <u>says</u> when he <u>sits</u> down at the table. "I don't like eating rice that's yellow!" Rebecca <u>looks</u> at Mark, and he <u>decides</u> to apologize to Ruth. Ruth <u>asks</u> him to try the rice first before telling her that he <u>hates</u> it. Mark <u>does</u>, and he <u>is</u> surprised because the rice <u>is</u> actually good!

Comprehension and Language Arts Skills

UNIT 6 A Changing America • **Lesson 6** *The California Gold Rush*

GRAMMAR AND USAGE

▶ **Future Tense**

▶ **Using Past, Present, and Future Tenses in Sentences**

Read the paragraph. Write the verb that is used to form the future tense in each blank.

"What _____ you cook for dinner tomorrow night,

Ruth?" Rebecca asked. "Mark and I _____ help you if you want us to."

   "That sounds like it _____ be a great idea," Ruth said.

"We _____ need to go to the store. I think I _____

try to make a new kind of rice. This time, the rice _____ have fish, garlic, and peas in it."

▶ **Past, Present, and Future Tense**

Read the sentences. Change the underlined verbs to the tense in parentheses. Write the new verb above the underlined verb.

1. We <u>cook</u> Ruth's new rice dish last night. She said that one

   <u>is</u> from Vietnam. (past tense)

2. Mark <u>says</u> that it <u>tastes</u> sweet, salty, and sour all at the same time. (past tense)

3. My favorite rice dish <u>came</u> from Haiti. It <u>had</u> red peppers in

   it, and it <u>was</u> so spicy that it <u>burned</u> my mouth! (present tense)

4. I still <u>liked</u> it, even though my mouth <u>felt</u> like it <u>was</u> on fire

   when I <u>ate</u> it. (present tense)

5. Ruth hopes that we <u>learn</u> a little bit about new people, places, and customs while we are enjoying our food. (future tense)

Charts, Graphs, and Tables

Charts, graphs and tables are visual presentations of information. Use them to present a lot of information in a small amount of space.

▶ There are many types of charts, tables and graphs. The following is an example of a **chart.** Charts contain rows and columns. Each row and column tells what type of information is in the chart.

Which foods do the birds like best?

	Suet	Millet	Peanut Hearts	Thistle	Cracked Corn
Blue Jay	x		x		
Finch	x			x	
Grosbeak	x				
Dove	x	x	x		x

▶ A **pie chart** is a circle that breaks things down into parts of a whole.

▶ A **bar graph** compares things or shows how something has changed.

What's in that Birdbrain Deluxe birdfood mixture?

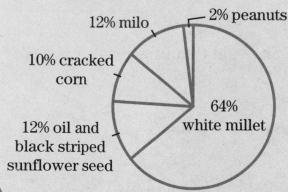

12% milo
2% peanuts
10% cracked corn
12% oil and black striped sunflower seed
64% white millet

Percentage of Schools with Internet Access

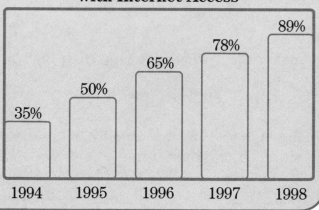

89% — 1998
78% — 1997
65% — 1996
50% — 1995
35% — 1994

Try It!　**Use the birdfeeding chart to answer these questions.**

1. Which birds like to eat millet? _____

2. What do finches like to eat? _____

3. What food do all the birds eat? _____

▶ Charts, Graphs, and Tables

Practice

Read the paragraph below. Turn the information into a chart or graph and give it a title.

This is information about major earthquakes in the United States in the 20th century. There was an earthquake in San Francisco, California, on April 18, 1906. It measured 7.7 on the Richter scale and caused 700 deaths. An earthquake in Prince William Sound, Alaska, on March 27, 1964, measured 9.2 on the Richter scale and caused 130 deaths. An earthquake in Yucca Valley, California, on June 28, 1992, measured 7.6 and caused one death.

WRITER'S CRAFT

UNIT 6 A Changing America • **Lesson 6** *The California Gold Rush*

Details in Descriptive Writing

Make your writing more interesting and vivid with descriptive details that help the reader experience the situation. Tell how things look, feel, taste, sound, or feel (to the touch). Don't just say the food was delicious or the dress was pretty. Tell exactly why it was delicious or beautiful. Be specific.

Rule	**Example**
▶ Use words that tell how things *look*.	▶ The Fourth of July fireworks burst into the black sky like giant green, blue, red, and silver flowers.
▶ Use words that tell how things *sound*.	▶ A few seconds after each burst of color, we could hear the booming explosion of the fireworks.
▶ Use words that tell how things *feel*.	▶ The ground beneath us shook from the force of the explosives.
▶ Use words that tell how things *smell or taste*.	▶ When the display was over, the smell of burning leaves filled the air. When we opened our mouths we could practically taste the bitter gunpowder.

 **Tell what senses the descriptions in each sentence use.**

1. No one wanted to enter the dark, shadowy room that

   smelled like rotting vegetables. _____

2. A green, foamy wave crashed against the rocks with a

   thunderous sound. _____

3. As soon as I entered the kitchen, my mouth watered for the

   chocolate cookies I could smell cooking in the oven. _____

▶ Details in Descriptive Writing

Practice

Imagine a favorite place, either indoors (restaurant, room, game arcade) or outdoors (the park, beach, woods). Close your eyes and picture being there. Then answer these questions.

4. What sounds do you hear? Describe the sounds. (For example, The electronic games clang and ring, and kids groan and cheer.)

_____

_____

5. What do you see in this place? Describe those things you see.

_____

_____

6. What things can you smell? Describe those smells.

_____

_____

7. Describe the way things feel against your hands or skin.

_____

_____

8. Describe anything you taste or eat in this place.

_____

_____

WRITER'S CRAFT

Cause and Effect

Focus   Understanding cause-and-effect relationships helps readers know what happens and why something happens in a story.

> Writers often use signal words and phrases to identify **cause-and-effect relationships.** These words include *because, so, if, then, thus, since, for,* and *therefore.*
> ▶ The **cause** is *why* something happens.
> ▶ The **effect** is *what* happens as a result.

Identify

Based on what you read in "The Golden Spike," fill in the spaces below with the cause or effect that completes the sentences.

1. Reporters from nearly every newspaper in the country were in Promontory, Utah, because

   _____

   _____.

2. The president of the Central Pacific was there also because

   _____

   _____.

3. _____

   _____

   the country became one.

Cause and Effect

Practice

Read the following sentences. Draw one line under the words that signal cause and two lines under the words that signal effect in each sentence.

4. The dog's fur was tangled, so we took her in for grooming.

5. Because it snowed all night, school was closed the following day.

6. The children played in the water because they were too hot to sit in the sun.

7. The trainer held the horse's reins since this was Maria's first time riding.

8. Since fast food restaurants have been introduced, meals at home have changed.

Apply

Think about something you did recently that you are proud of. Write a short paragraph about what made you proud. Use words and sentences that show a cause-and-effect relationship.

_____

_____

_____

_____

_____

_____

_____

_____

COMPREHENSION

Review

Capitalization and Punctuation

Read the paragraph. Correct any capitalization or punctuation errors. Use proofreading marks to make the corrections.

the united states and japan fought during world war II On december 7 1941 japanese planes bombed the pearl harbor naval base in hawaii. after the attack on pearl harbor the us government ordered everyone who looked like they were japanese to leave their houses and report to places called internment camps. japanese-americans werent happy about this at all many of them had been born in the united states or they had become american citizens they hadnt even done anything wrong but the government said that didnt matter.

Parts of Speech

Read the sentences. Circle all of the nouns. Underline all of the verbs. Draw a box or a square around all of the pronouns. Draw an X through each adjective, and underline each adverb twice.

1. The government did not hurt or injure the people who lived in the internment camps, but they were not allowed to leave until the United States gave them permission to go home.

2. The camps were hot and crowded, and soldiers watched everyone twenty-four hours a day.

3. Children had not been allowed to bring many toys, games, or books with them, because their families were told to leave their houses quickly.

4. They talked and played outdoor games while the adults talked to each other too.

UNIT 6 A Changing America • **Lesson 7** *The Golden Spike*

► **Clauses and Phrases**

Read the sentences. Write an A over each appositive phrase, the letters PA over each participial phrase, and the letters PR over each prepositional phrase. Circle each dependent clause, underline each adjective clause, and draw a box or a square around each adverb clause.

5. Many years later, people began to tell the government that it should apologize to the Japanese-Americans who had lived in the camps.

6. In the United States, a person can't be punished for doing something unless a judge or jury says that person has committed a crime.

7. Agreeing that it should apologize, the government decided to send a letter and some money to the people who had to live in the camps.

► **Kinds and Types of Sentences**

Read the sentences. Write *simple, compound,* or *complex* and *declarative, exclamatory, interrogative,* or *imperative* to describe what kind of sentence each one is.

8. Martin Luther King, Jr., gave a very famous speech in Washington, and he asked people of all races and cultures to treat each other fairly. _____

9. Please tell me the name of this speech. _____

10. Do any of your relatives remember hearing it on TV or on the radio? _____

GRAMMAR, USAGE, AND MECHANICS

Organization of Descriptive Writing

When you are describing a place, thing, or even a person, you can write your description using *top-to-bottom* or *left-to-right* organization to help the reader see what you are describing.

Rule

▶ Place and location words help readers see where things are in your descriptions.

▶ For things that are mostly vertical, such as a person standing, describe them using top-to-bottom (or bottom-to-top) organization.

▶ For things that are mostly horizontal, such as an automobile or things in a room, describe them using left-to-right (or right-to-left) organization.

Examples

▶ Here are some examples of place and location words.

above   below   beside   on

across   under   over   near

▶ Jared has black curly hair. His eyes are dark brown, and he has a cute button nose.

▶ On the left side of the room is my desk with my computer on it. Next to the desk stands a black floor lamp. On the right side of my room is a chair I throw all my clothes on.

 **Try It!** Underline the place and location words and write which type of organization is used in the paragraph.

Mom told me to rearrange the shelves so my one-year-old brother couldn't get into trouble. She said to put the breakable things like glasses and dishes on the top shelf and the unbreakable dishes and cups on the middle shelf. She told me to put the things he could play with on the bottom shelf.

What type of organization is used in this paragraph?

_____

UNIT 6 A Changing America • **Lesson 7** *The Golden Spike*

Organization of Descriptive Writing

Practice

Draw a line through the word or words that are *not* place and location words.

when	beside	soon	similarly	anyway	across
next to	on	outside	top	bottom	front

Write a short paragraph describing how to get to your school classroom from the main entrance.

_____

_____

_____

_____

_____

_____

_____

_____

_____

_____

_____

_____

_____

_____

_____

WRITER'S CRAFT